NEW DIRECTIONS FOR TEACHING AND LEARNING

Robert J. Menges, *Northwestern University*
EDITOR-IN-CHIEF

Marilla D. Svinicki, *University of Texas, Austin*
ASSOCIATE EDITOR

Student Self-Evaluation: Fostering Reflective Learning

Jean MacGregor
The Evergreen State College

EDITOR

Number 56, Winter 1993

JOSSEY-BASS PU~~~~~~~
San Francisco

D1468948

STUDENT SELF-EVALUATION: FOSTERING REFLECTIVE LEARNING
Jean MacGregor (ed.)
New Directions for Teaching and Learning, no. 56
Robert J. Menges, Editor-in-Chief
Marilla D. Svinicki, Associate Editor

Microfilm copies of issues and articles are available in 16mm and 35mm, as well as microfiche in 105mm, through University Microfilms Inc., 300 North Zeeb Road, Ann Arbor, Michigan 48106-1346.

LC 85-644763   ISSN 0271-0633   ISBN 1-55542-683-2

NEW DIRECTIONS FOR TEACHING AND LEARNING is part of The Jossey-Bass Higher and Adult Education Series and is published quarterly by Jossey-Bass Inc., Publishers, 350 Sansome Street, San Francisco, California 94104-1342. Second-class postage paid at San Francisco, California, and at additional mailing offices. POSTMASTER: Send address changes to New Directions for Teaching and Learning, Jossey-Bass Inc., Publishers, 350 Sansome Street, San Francisco, California 94104-1342.

SUBSCRIPTIONS for 1993 cost $47.00 for individuals and $62.00 for institutions, agencies, and libraries.

EDITORIAL CORRESPONDENCE should be sent to Robert J. Menges, Northwestern University, Center for the Teaching Professions, 2003 Sheridan Road, Evanston, Illinois 60208-2610.

Cover photograph by Richard Blair/Color & Light © 1990.

Manufactured in the United States of America. Nearly all Jossey-Bass books, jackets, and periodicals are printed on recycled paper that contains at least 50 percent recycled waste, including 10 percent postconsumer waste. Many of our materials are also printed with vegetable-based ink; during the printing process these inks emit fewer volatile organic compounds (VOCs) than petroleum-based inks. VOCs contribute to the formation of smog.

CONTENTS

EDITOR'S NOTES

For several decades, college teachers have been asking students to engage in self-evaluation, to reflect on their academic work and describe and evaluate it in writing. Student self-evaluation is both a process—consisting of acts of reflecting, composing, and writing—and a product, a written document. Neither the process nor the product obviate the need for student exams and papers, which are crucial indicators of student mastery of material or complexity of thinking. Rather, student self-evaluation supplements and complements that information by asking students to describe in their own words their learning and its value to them. This writing, and the conversations that faculty members and students have about it, can be instructional, illuminating, at times even transformative.

Student self-evaluation is both an old approach and a new one. It has a long history in alternative colleges. Faculty members there have always wanted to evaluate their students more extensively and qualitatively than they could by assigning grades, and at the same time they have wanted—and expected—students to claim the value and meaning of their learning in their own words. At more traditional institutions as well, some faculty have engaged their students in self-evaluation and have encouraged the active participation of their students in the process.

More recent initiatives in undergraduate education create a rich and more complex rationale for self-reflection and self-assessment of one's learning; a growing body of student self-evaluation practice is springing up in nearly every discipline. Learning theorists are advocating the value of having students think more consciously (or "metacognitively") about their learning and thinking. Scholars of student and young-adult development are suggesting that we cannot separate the development of "voice," or a personal sense of agency, from the development of self and mind. Educators in the professions contend that the skills and habits of critical reflection are pillars of effective professional practice. Moreover, the burgeoning national interest in assessment of student learning has spawned a rich array of practice, as in focus groups, portfolio evaluation, and "classroom research" (Angelo and Cross, 1993). All these student-centered assessment strategies bring student perspectives into the assessment conversation.

Student self-evaluation is primarily a learning strategy, but it is also a promising assessment approach: While enriching learning for students, student self-evaluations also can help teachers and institutions learn about student learning. This volume introduces the many forms of student self-evaluation in undergraduate teaching settings and describes how it creates connections between learners and learning, knowers and the known, and the self and the mind.

Some points of distinction are necessary. In this volume we will be focusing on self-evaluation as narrative writing, not on self-evaluation in the sense of self-grading (students proposing for themselves the grade they think they deserve for a class). The form of self-evaluation discussed here involves students in describing their learning and making qualitative judgments about it. Second, student self-evaluation concerns itself with learning and meaning-making in college courses; this work should not be confused with self-revelatory writing or personal self-disclosure for therapeutic purposes. Third, we will be using the term student self-evaluation (lower case) generally to mean the process of writing student self-evaluations and Student Self-Evaluation (upper case), or the acronym SSE, generally to mean the written products or documents that students produce. Fourth, some readers might wonder about our using the term *student self-evaluation* instead of *student self-assessment*. We are using the term *self-evaluation* for two reasons. It has been in use at several of the authors' colleges (Antioch University, Seattle; Fairhaven College at Western Washington University; and The Evergreen State College) over several decades and has long-standing meaning on each campus for students, faculty, and administrators. In addition, as a practice, it arose as an alternative to traditional letter or number grades and has been central to these colleges' systems of evaluating students. The term *student self-assessment* is more recent and connotes processes that stand alongside traditional evaluative systems and provide informal or formal information about student learning to students, faculty members, or others involved in either classroom-based or campuswide assessment work. Occasionally in this volume, the terms *self-evaluation* and *self-assessment* are interchangeable, but usually one term or the other best fits a particular context.

Chapter One introduces self-evaluation and describes the qualities teachers look for in this kind of reflective writing. The authors, Edith Kusnic and Mary Lou Finley, find confirmation of the processes and outcomes of student self-evaluation in the ideas of major learning theorists. In Chapter Two, Carl Waluconis provides an overview of various contexts in which teachers ask students to write self-evaluations, from short in-class writing exercises all the way to formal Summary and Evaluation papers that span a student's entire undergraduate career. For almost all students, self-evaluation is an unfamiliar and challenging process at first. In Chapter Three, I describe some of the difficulties students encounter as they first write self-evaluations, and I suggest some strategies to help students build familiarity and fluency. Marie Eaton and Rita Pougiales further explore the conditions that support self-evaluation in Chapter Four and spell out the implications of this kind of teaching for student autonomy and authority.

Student self-evaluations are just beginning to be seen as valuable in the assessment of college outcomes. In Chapter Five, William Moore and Steve Hunter argue for including student voices in assessment work. They report on several assessment students in Washington State that have focused on SSE documents. Chapter Six, by Richard Haswell, returns to Chapter One's claim that student self-evaluation supports student development and explores whether student self-evaluation might even induce development. Haswell closes the volume by suggesting that student self-evaluation offers teachers a model "for other educational ways to convert their students' education into an experience that will not be lost but will end up part of their students' lives." An appendix provides sample student self-evaluation assignments, sample SSE essays, and a short bibliography of resources.

This book grew out of the work of an informal working group on student self-evaluation in Washington State that was sponsored by the Washington Center for Improving Undergraduate Education. Since the mid-1980s, the Washington Center has promoted both the development of learning community programs (strategies for clustering courses around interdisciplinary themes and enrolling common groups of students) and various approaches to collaborative teaching and learning. A number of campuses in Washington have become involved in these efforts, and the Washington Center has provided a forum for sharing not only promising curricula and teaching approaches but assessment approaches as well. Moreover, the support of Washington's Higher Education Coordinating Board and State Board for Community and Technical Colleges for campus-based approaches to outcomes assessment helped to create a climate of innovation and inter-institutional collaboration. Following a working conference on student self-evaluation in 1990, the nine authors of this volume continued to meet—first to share approaches to student self-evaluation and then to share and critique drafts of these chapters. We come from different institutional contexts and use self-evaluation in different ways but have found common ground in our assumptions and intentions, our successes and our dilemmas. In writing this book collaboratively, we experienced much of what students do in self-evaluation, working simultaneously on the strands of synthesis and description of our work and on personal reflection and evaluation.

As we assembled this book, we drew on the generosity of many colleagues who shared their work and insights. We are especially grateful to Kirk Thompson for his path-breaking research and writing about SSEs at The Evergreen State College. Although we have primarily drawn on the work in self-evaluation in Washington State, we acknowledge that faculty members elsewhere are using self-evaluation in a growing variety of undergraduate settings. For their insights on their own experiences with student self-evaluation, we thank Les Adler (the Hutchins School at Sonoma State University), Thad Curtz (The Evergreen State College), Will Hamlin (Goddard College), Jackie Moorey (Antioch University, Seattle), Steve Sharkey and Judy Reisetter (Alverno College), and Kathleen Taylor (St. Mary's College of California). The following faculty members shared not only their experiences but also many examples of SSEs from their classes: Catharine Beyer, Joan Graham, Debbie Hatch, and Kim Johnson-Bogart (all with the Interdisciplinary Writing Program at the University of Washington), Don Foran (Centralia College), Bruce Kochis (North Seattle

Community College), Ánne Martin and Pat Nerison (Edmonds Community College), Judy Moore and Eric Mould (Yakima Valley Community College), Dwight Oberholtzer (Pacific Lutheran University), Kathleen O'Brian (Alverno College), Claudia Questo (Green River Community College), Jan Ray and Bobby Righi (Seattle Central Community College), Sarah Recken (Washington State University), and Jerry Zimmerman (Lower Columbia College). We are deeply grateful to these teachers and to their students, who gave us permission to quote them. Finally, special thanks go to additional individuals who read and criticized our first drafts of this manuscript: Cindy Avens, Valerie Bystrom, Seth Frankel, Chris Kellett, Roberta Matthews, Rebecca Montgomery, Linda Reisser, Sam Schrager, Barbara Leigh Smith, Kathleen Taylor, Nancy Taylor, and Richard Zelley. The interest, experiences, and good advice of all of these individuals strengthened our collaborative endeavor and enriched it as well.

Jean MacGregor
Editor

Reference

Angelo, T. A., and Cross, K. P. *Classroom Assessment Techniques: A Handbook for College Teachers.* (2nd ed.) San Francisco: Jossey-Bass, 1993.

JEAN MACGREGOR is associate director of the Washington Center for Improving the Quality of Undergraduate Education, a public service initiative of The Evergreen State College. The Washington Center is a consortium of forty-four colleges in Washington State working simultaneously on curriculum improvement, faculty development, and assessment.

Student self-evaluation is a powerful learning tool for students that can help faculty members directly achieve the outcomes and purposes they intend in educational practice.

Student Self-Evaluation: An Introduction and Rationale

Edith Kusnic, Mary Lou Finley

In "The Aims of Education," Alfred North Whitehead advises us to "beware of inert ideas that are merely received into the mind without being utilized, or tested, or thrown into fresh combinations. By utilizing an idea, I mean relating it to that stream, compounded of sense perceptions, feelings, hopes, desires, and of mental activities adjusting thought to thought, which forms our life" ([1929] 1949, p. 13). Whitehead asserts, "Education is the art of the utilization of knowledge." As educators we must help students develop this art: to throw ideas into fresh combinations, make ideas part of their lives, make meaning from them, use them. Self-evaluation has the power to help students achieve the kind of learning Whitehead encouraged and, in addition, to support other kinds of growth and development.

Educators have long understood the importance of self-reflection, and the resultant personal development, as central to the college experience. However, this important work is generally deemed the responsibility of the "student life" sector of the campus, with the staff of counseling centers, placement offices, or residence halls providing assistance to students and helping them reflect on their undergraduate experiences. Student life activities and residence hall experiences do create a climate that fosters reflection; they certainly did for both of us during our own undergraduate careers. Today, however, most students do not have access to dormitory life or even a facsimile of it. In fact, fewer and fewer students attend college as residential students. Many attend community colleges or commute to four-year institutions. Increasing numbers of students are working adults whose lives preclude the opportunity for extensive self-reflective conversations with other students. In this kind of environment, new strategies are needed. Student self-evaluation is one strategy for developing skills of self-reflection, bringing students more fully into the educational process, and helping them build active and meaningful relationships with the material they are studying.

For more than seven years, we have been teaching and advising adults returning to college in an undergraduate completion program at Antioch University, Seattle. Student self-evaluative writing is at the heart of a student's program of study: in courses, degree-planning documents, prior-learning documents, formal documents called Quarterly Student Self-Assessments, and summative self-evaluations prior to graduation. The following two passages, written by first-quarter students at Antioch who have had opportunities to write reflectively and self-evaluatively, suggest the power of such work:

> When I began the quarter, I felt incredibly lost. . . . I was in a constant state of panic at the thought of being in school again and not being able to keep up with my work. While I am starting to believe that the last of these concerns is a part of being a student again, I do feel quite a shift in how I view myself as a student.
>
> In the reflective essays that I have written for [this course], I have developed a stronger sense of what I have accomplished in the past and how those things are useful to me now. The readings have challenged me to question why I believe what I believe in many cases. This is not to say that I always changed my viewpoint on important issues simply because of the readings and essays. It is more to say that I examined my thoughts more closely and adjusted my opinions when I felt new ideas had meaning to me and justified incorporation into my mind-set. [Quarterly Self-Assessment, first-quarter Antioch student]

> I've learned more about being a student and what it means to learn. I used to think being a student was the single most terrible thing that I could be. Learning something meant studying something. Study meant memorize. It had no meaning. No wonder, I couldn't remember anything. I had no way to see its purpose in my life.
>
> The single greatest thing that I can say for my experiences as a student this time is that the information has meaning. It doesn't just have meaning because I had to learn it. It had meaning because I got to "pick it up, turn it around, and ask questions about it." [Quarterly Self-Assessment, first-quarter Antioch student]

As they progress in their work at Antioch and reflect on the nature, quality, and substance of their learning, students strengthen their skills of analysis, synthesis, and evaluation; work to make sense of what they have learned and explore its relationship to their previous knowledge and ideas; become more conscious of their values and more cognizant of the ways in which they form values; deepen their learning and build connections between themselves and the content of their studies; and develop the skills, competence, and authority required for effective lifelong learning. Student self-evaluation is a powerful tool for helping students integrate their knowledge of the world with knowledge of themselves and build a foundation of confidence, knowledge, and commitment from which to act as individuals, professionals, and citizens.

The following passage suggests how a more advanced student is able to support claims with evidence, synthesize ideas, and use that synthesis to help her understand her life. It also shows her ability to evaluate the level and quality of learning she has achieved through a particular course and suggests her right to decide which learning is most important for her:

> [In this course] there was another aspect of learning taking place on a consciously-directed level. I read about and compared Erikson's, Breger's, and, to a lesser extent, Piaget's maps of childhood development and noticed a development, in the theories themselves, towards viewing the child as increasingly more autonomous, complex and inner-directed. In learning about these theories, I applied them to my own childhood, in retrospect, and analyzed my own stages of development, the conflicts inherent in each and the degree to which I have, or have not, resolved them. This level of learning is demonstrated both in my weekly essays and my journal, as well as my participation in class discussions. On the other hand, I would be hard-pressed to reiterate these theories in more than the most general terms; I can say I have an understanding of the material, but not a command of it. My level of learning may be assessed more optimistically in the insights I have gained about my own childhood—a very personal value, important to me. [End-of-course SSE, advanced Antioch student]

Certainly not every student grows in all the ways reflected in this extract. A few write Self-Evaluations as a rote exercise and do not change in noticeable ways at all. However, because of what we have witnessed, we are excited about the potential of student self-evaluation as an educational tool.

Student self-evaluation also provides a new form of feedback. It can create an opportunity for dialogue about student learning between student and teacher, student and adviser, and perhaps even student and larger institution. We learn what keeps students motivated, engaged, and interested and what they experience as important learning. What we hear may raise important questions about teaching and learning in the classroom: What we think we are teaching is not what students are learning; what we think is clear and simple is, instead, complex and troubling; what we say is heard differently by different students. A mechanism that gives us access to students' ideas about their own learning allows us to provide sounder and more effective educational experiences. Furthermore, student self-evaluation can provide useful data for outcomes assessment.

Some colleges have fully integrated self-evaluation into the entire institution; in others, self-evaluation is used in a few classes. Different uses may create different outcomes. Regardless of its scope, faculty members have a common understanding of the usefulness and potential of student self-evaluation.

To encourage additional faculty and institutions to incorporate student self-evaluation into their educational practice, we begin here by describing more fully what we mean by student self-evaluation and then explore the underlying mental acts of reflection and self-reflection. We also summarize the qualities that emerge in student self-evaluations and identify some key ideas from developmental and educational theory that reinforce the rationale for student self-evaluation.

Student Self-Evaluation: Context and Definition

During the past twenty-five years, there has been considerable experimentation with student self-evaluation. The term *student self-evaluation* refers to different things depending on where and how it is used. Student self-evaluation appears in classroom assignments: journal writing, short writing assignments in which students are asked to write about what they learned in one particular class session, or synthesis/reflection papers written during the course or at the end of a term. Some colleges that grant credit for prior experiential learning (learning gained through life and work experiences) include some type of self-evaluative, reflective writing as part of the documentation process. Growing numbers of colleges require some sort of summative, evaluative essay to accompany a student's portfolio for a course. Several campuses also incorporate more formal student self-evaluations periodically throughout a student's academic career or as a summative evaluation before graduation; these sometimes become part of the student's files or formal transcripts.

The term *student self-evaluation* refers to both a written product, which can take a variety of forms, and to the process that produces such pieces of student writing. As process, student self-evaluation asks students to think and write about what they have learned. Student self-evaluation as process is a powerful learning tool. As products, student self-evaluations describe and analyze students' learning for themselves and for us.

In all these different uses, students reflect on what they have learned—describing it in qualitative terms, synthesizing it, making sense of it, and evaluating it. Thus we offer the following definition: Student self-evaluation is the student's reflection on and evaluation of his or her learning, in writing, seen as an integral part of the learning experience in educational settings. By writing about what they have learned, students are asked, in Whitehead's terms, to utilize ideas—to make them their own. Student self-evaluation offers students an opportunity to put themselves at the center of the learning experience. Because of its written nature, student self-evaluation calls on the demanding skills of thought and self-representation. And because it is part of what students do in educational settings, it is validated as important and valuable. Student self-evaluation is not a substitute for tests, term papers, or other forms of evaluating student learning. Rather, it supplements them, providing the instructor or adviser with additional evaluative information.

Reflection and Self-Reflection: Keys to Student Self-Evaluation

We are all familiar with the kind of reflection required in essay exams or student papers. We may ask students to compare and contrast points of view, present their own analysis of a work of art or historical event, or explore the implications of a particular theory. We are interested in their critical thinking skills, their mastery of a given body of knowledge, their ability to support their opinions with evidence, and their ability to see connections between the world of ideas and the everyday world. In these traditional kinds of assignments, students have to draw together different elements of what they have learned to explore a topic or answer a question. At their best, essays and research papers help students organize a collection of information and ideas and transform them into something clear and coherent.

Student self-evaluation often includes this familiar kind of reflective thinking, but it adds new dimensions. It asks students to cultivate the art of reflection consciously and intentionally, to be aware that they are reflecting. In the first example of student self-evaluative writing cited in this chapter, we can see this self-consciousness about the importance of reflective thinking. The student asserts that through her reflective writing she became a more effective student.

Student self-evaluation requires not only reflection but also self-reflection. Students are asked to think not only about what they have learned but also about what they have learned in relation to themselves. Their own subjectivity as learners and knowers is brought into the educational arena. Inviting the student's developing self into the educational enterprise helps him or her to build a relationship with the subject matter. We get a glimpse of this process at work in the third example cited above, in which the student describes beginning to grasp theories of child development because she had an opportunity to connect these theories to her own childhood. Her self-evaluation reveals that the opportunity helped her begin to transform her learning from a passive process to an active, meaningful one.

Qualities of Student Self-Evaluation

When students are asked to write about what they have learned, there is, predictably, a range of responses. Advanced students who have had more practice may offer more complex analyses of their learning and richer descriptions of its meaning and relevance. More introspective students may be better equipped to reflect on the personal dimensions of their experience.

In spite of these differences, student self-evaluations demonstrate six important qualities. Not every example of student self-evaluative writing necessarily demonstrates all six. Naturally, what emerges is likely to be influenced by what students are asked. Nevertheless, the following qualities are central to the process of self-evaluation: an attitude of inquiry, integration of learning, meaning and relevance, voice and authority, self-directedness, and learning as a transaction between self and world.

An attitude of inquiry. When we ask students to move beyond what Whitehead called "inert ideas" and ask them to have an active relationship with the material, they are no longer only passive recipients of the ideas of others. They are challenged to see the assumptions and implications of the course material. Such an attitude of active inquiry cultivates critical thinking.

Integration of learning. When we ask students to inquire more actively into ideas and information in course material, they may begin to integrate what they have learned with learning from other courses, with their previous understanding of the topic, or with their own experience. They can begin to synthesize their knowledge. Sometimes this integration process goes smoothly, with new material clarifying previous understandings. At other times the process may seem tumultuous, as new perspectives conflict with previous ideas. The act of writing frequently helps to sort out the issues and to further this process of integration.

Meaning and relevance. The student's effort to integrate new learning helps to illuminate the meaning of that learning to the student. As we ask students to explore the meaning they make from their learning experiences, they frequently begin to understand its relevance to their lives, work, and ways of relating to the world. They may begin to see how the ideas have application in practical situations or can be used to make sense out of their own experiences; they may begin to integrate theory and practice. Ideas take on meaning; meaning creates a sense of relevance; relevance creates the motivation to apply the ideas in one's life.

Voice and authority. Through the workings of the previous three qualities, we often see students begin to develop and exercise their own "voices" (see Belenky, Clinchy, Goldberger, and Tarule, 1986) and assume greater authority for what they know. When we ask them to name what they know and form an opinion of its quality, meaning, and relevance, students are challenged to be articulate about what they have learned and the meaning they have made of it. Because student self-evaluation provides an external audience for the student's reflections—whether that be teachers, advisers, or administrators—their right to speak and have an opinion is validated. This external validation by those in authority in an educational setting (faculty), encourages students to assume greater authority for what they have learned and what they know.

Self-directedness. As students assume greater authority for their learning, they identify the questions that emerge for them through their studies and find themselves drawn to further exploration of certain topics. They plan and take control of the course of their future learning. In addition, evaluating what they have learned helps students be conscious of themselves as learners. When we ask them to identify strengths and weaknesses in their learning, students begin to understand how to become better learners.

Learning as a transaction between self and world. When students claim authority over the content, process, and direction of their education, they begin to connect more actively with the world outside themselves. The interests and questions they follow through their studies may help guide their choice of a career or provide greater understanding of how social or cultural conditions have influenced their behavior and attitudes. They experience learning as a transaction between themselves and the world and strengthen their capacity to see themselves as agents of effective action.

Student self-evaluation, then, creates an interactive environment—between the student and teacher, between the learner and the learning, between learning and knowledge. It can help create meaning and relevance for learners and thus increase engagement, ownership, and motivation. It can strengthen students' critical thinking skills and strengthen their "voices"—thus providing a basis for them to claim authority for their learning and knowledge. It can bring students into an arena we might call the community of learned persons—people capable of forming and substantiating opinions, thinking for themselves and participating in the shaping of their lives and their worlds. Taken together, these qualities can create learning outcomes that meet the commonly stated purposes of higher education: the development of confident, self-directed learners capable of learning continuously from their work and their lives.

At its best, student self-evaluation makes learning real to students. All learning is about change: about changing the way we see things and changing the skills we have to new and different ones. In self-evaluative writing, students are asked to be more self-conscious about the changes they are experiencing intellectually, personally, and in their relationship with people and ideas outside themselves. Self-evaluation becomes a means of assisting the development of the student as a whole person, including their emotional, spiritual, and value-driven aspects as well as their intellectual selves. By paying attention to what students say in self-evaluations, we can more appropriately guide their learning and development.

Learning and Development

As we have read students' self-reflective writing, we have tried to learn what students need and how we can help them. To help us make sense of what they tell us, we have sought clues from several educational theorists, who have confirmed and illuminated our understanding of both the process and products of student self-evaluation.

Benjamin Bloom (1969) considers analysis, synthesis, and evaluation the higher-level thinking skills that compose "critical thinking." Student self-evaluation, in its most comprehensive form, asks students to use these higher-order thinking skills as they analyze what they have learned, identify key components, compare and contrast ideas, discern themes and make judgments, and construct meaning. The development of complex thinking abilities and meaning-making is also the focus of William Perry's work (1970). The Perry scheme of student intellectual development in college reflects two interwoven dynamics: (1) students' confronting and coping with diversity and uncertainty and (2) the attendant evolution of meaning-making about learning, authority (the teacher), and self. Student self-evaluation illuminates, and may even stimulate, development in the ways Perry describes, particularly if used summatively and episodically.

Two sets of ideas have been particularly helpful for understanding the potential of student self-evaluation in relation to students' psychological and social development. First, Carl Rogers (1969) advocates educational approaches concerned with the learner as a whole person. He also focuses on the meaning-making process, especially in terms of the authority relationship between student and teacher and the relationship of both to identity development. Rogers's perspective lends support to student self-evaluation as a strategy for encouraging "significant, meaningful, experiential learning." We ask students to focus on the relationship between themselves and the material studied, to judge the extent to which ideas are substantiated in their own experience, and to identify which learning is significant to them.

Second, Belenky, Clinchy, Goldberger, and Tarule (1986), the authors of Women's Ways of Knowing, present a framework of epistemological development derived from their research on women learners. They explore identity development as the foundation for creating meaning and purpose, forming and clarifying values, and being able to act effectively. The metaphor of "voice" appears throughout the book, stressing the links between identity development and intellectual development. Student self-evaluation explicitly asks students to acknowledge this interconnection by bringing themselves and their identities into their education.

John Dewey and David Kolb both note the important role reflection plays in the learning process. Dewey (1938) describes reflective thinking as the capacity to stand back from experience, look at it, and make sense of it in the context of past experiences and previous knowledge. For Dewey, developing this capacity is a central purpose of education. Kolb (1984) extends Dewey's ideas by describing learning as a circular process. Information from both subjective and objective sources flows into us, is processed into new knowledge through interaction with our previous store of knowledge, and flows back into the world in action. In this way, human learning can be seen as an act of engagement, the basic human transaction that links the individual and the world. When we add student self-evaluation to our instructional repertoire, we intentionally provide students with the opportunity for conscious reflection. We make a place for students to articulate their subjective relationship with course material and therefore to conceive of learning as a much more active process than merely taking in information. It is also what one does with what one takes in, how one makes sense of it, values it, or expresses it.

Finally, for Brazilian educator Paulo Freire (1970), the intellectual act of reflection builds the capacity for authenticity and dialogue, which are key prerequisites of freedom. By naming their own experience of the world and solving real problems in their lives, Freire argues, individuals validate their authenticity as human beings and begin to understand their experience and create the conditions for changing their experience in the ways they desire. Through self-evaluation assignments, we pose students' own learning as a problem to be solved. We challenge students to name and validate their own experience and to create a more conscious sense of their authentic selves.

Conclusion

Self-evaluation is a learning strategy that helps students make meaning, derive relevance, and build coherence through their educational experiences. This form of active engagement seems an important antidote to passivity in the classroom. It is an especially important strategy for particular populations of students: older students, students of color, women, and students with more divergent or active learning styles. Often these students need to find ways to link traditional academic perspectives to their own experience and concerns. In addition, older adult students usually have fully formed opinions and substantial experience that must be integrated with new learning if the new learning is to have value.

We have found that faculty members need to approach students' self-evaluative writing as learners, listening to what students say and trying to understand what it means for our work as teachers and advisers. Understanding the dimensions of student development helps us to become more reflective ourselves and to be more effective guides for student learning and growth. Furthermore, we can learn to help students use their education to, in Whitehead's terms, learn "the art of the utilization of knowledge."

References

Belenky, M. F., Clinchy, B. M., Goldberger, N. R., and Tarule, J. M. *Women's Ways of Knowing: The Development of Self, Voice, and Mind.* New York: Basic Books, 1986.

Bloom, B. *Taxonomy of Educational Objectives.* New York: McKay, 1969.

Dewey, J. *Experience and Education.* Toronto, Ontario: Collier-Macmillan Canada, 1938.

Freire, P. *Pedagogy of the Oppressed.* New York: Seabury Press, 1970.

Kolb, D. A. *Experiential Learning: Experience as the Source of Learning and Development.* Englewood Cliffs, N.J.: Prentice Hall, 1984.

Perry, W. G. *Forms of Intellectual and Ethical Development in the College Years: A Scheme.* Troy, Mo.: Holt, Rinehart & Winston, 1970.

Rogers, C. R. *Freedom to Learn.* Columbus, Ohio: Merrill, 1969.

Whitehead, A. N. *The Aims of Education and Other Essays.* New York: Mentor Books, 1949. (Originally published 1929.)

EDITH KUSNIC is a core faculty member in the B.A. Completion Program at Antioch University, Seattle, Washington.

MARY LOU FINLEY is a core faculty member in the B.A. Completion Program at Antioch University, Seattle, Washington.

Student self-evaluations are used in a variety of classroom settings, formal and informal. Student self-reflective writing can be stimulated in a number of ways.

Self-Evaluation: Settings and Uses

Carl J. Waluconis

Faculty members ask students to write student self-evaluations (SSEs) in myriad settings and contexts. The writing that results provides a window on student learning in a variety of disciplines. Students are asked to write SSEs at different times in their academic careers: when they enter an institution, midway through a learning experience, or as a summative effort at the end. The context in which students write SSEs affects their view of the essays as formal or informal and their focus on self-evaluation as a process or product.

Even a quick overview of the different contexts in which students write self-evaluations creates a substantial list. However, this listing does not pretend to be comprehensive. Its purpose is to draw a picture of how and when teachers may use student self-evaluation, what may be contained in the writing, and what students may focus on and realize in their self-reflection. Because the context in which self-evaluation occurs helps determine how to assign or respond to SSEs, and whether or not to grade them, this chapter deals with those related issues as well.

For students, SSEs can be a simple record of learning and the act of writing one a moment of accountability, but at their best SSEs are also a process of self-discovery. As students articulate their own understanding of their learning, something happens. They begin to construct the meaning of what they did. Frequently student self-evaluation becomes an "epistemic" writing experience: Through the writing, something is discovered that was not clearly seen before. Student self-evaluation is an avenue for students to construct the meaning of what they did and describe new insights. Students often express appreciation for the experience and point out its value. "I wouldn't have looked at this if you hadn't asked" and "This is not an ending but an opening up of a process that can continue" are the sort of comments that teachers frequently hear from students about their SSEs.

Additionally, whether short or long, informal or formal, SSEs provide teachers with a wealth of information. SSEs provide a picture of where our teaching practices may be overchallenging or underchallenging students and where our practices may be inhibiting rather than promoting students' progress (Taylor and Marienau, 1993). SSEs illuminate how students are learning to be learners in our disciplines, as well as what stands out as meaningful, exciting, or perplexing.

Contexts for Student Self-Evaluations

Because student self-evaluation occurs in so many different contexts, a variety of methods for student self-evaluation are available to teachers. Differences in institutional settings cause some of this variety. The variety in student self-evaluation also reflects differences between disciplines or differences between individual faculty members. However, the methods of different institutions, different disciplines, and different faculty often overlap, and so it is problematic to use these distinctions for categorizing the contexts of student self-evaluation. Rather, differentiating contexts on the basis of the slice of student time on which self-evaluation focuses may be more useful.

SSEs Focusing on Work in a Brief Period. On the "micro" end of the SSE spectrum are the very valuable one-minute papers suggested as a "classroom research" strategy by Angelo and Cross (1993). At the end of class, students generate a few sentences about the most valuable aspect of the class and the most confusing or problematic. These notes from students provide faculty with an immediate look at student perspectives and questions about the class, and they furnish students an opportunity to reflect systematically on their own learning. At Edmonds Community College (Lynnwood, Washington), for example, faculty members frequently ask students to write brief reflections about their participation in student-centered book seminars. At the conclusion of a seminar on Leslie Silko's *Ceremony,* a student wrote,

> I found myself becoming engulfed in parts of this seminar with strong emotions, sometimes even with a sense of rage. This is probably greatly because of my own experience with prejudice and isolation . . . and this came out in my energy in seminar. [One-minute paper, Edmonds Community College]

The short SSE may also be used for discussion between faculty and students concerning their preparation for a larger writing assignment. At Edmonds Community College, faculty members ask students if their opinions changed while preparing to write an essay arguing whether, how much, and what kinds of prejudice exists. One student noted,

> It really surprised me that racism/prejudice is right here, right now. . . . Why are [unaccepting people] so afraid? There are strengths in differences,

not weaknesses. [One-minute paper, English composition student, Edmonds Community College]

For the same assignment, another student wrote,

Also in writing the essay, I found some interesting things during the interviews and speakers that I didn't know previously which didn't really change how I felt, but rather helped me see that although I knew a little about a subject, there was still a lot that I didn't know. [English composition student, Edmonds Community College]

In writing classes, teachers are increasingly asking students to write SSEs of the writing process immediately after writing papers. Michael Allen and Barbara Roswell (1989) have coined the term *post-write* for this method of self-assessment and offer the following as an example:

Now that you have finished your essay, please answer the following questions. There are no right or wrong answers. We are interested in your analysis of your experience writing this essay.

What problems did you face during the writing of this essay?
First, I had a problem deciding which side I was on. I tried to go without being biased. Second, I had a problem limiting my thesis to just "education is needed."

What solutions did you find for these problems?
I listed the pro and cons of basketball playing to get a feel for my opinions. Why is it good? Why is it bad? Then I thought about each part to take my point of view. In this way I could view both sides of the argument and still side with one. When I did this, my thesis became clear, unified, and restricted. . . .

. . . *Imagine you had more time to write this essay. What would you do if you were to continue working on it?*
My diction could be better. Such as "the players who do not make it pro." I could have said "the players who don't become professional"—less words and easier to say. [Post-write, writing student, Goucher College, quoted in Allen and Roswell, 1989, p. 16]

The complete post-write assignment is included in the appendix. Asking students to pay systematic attention to their writing problems and their strategies for solving them, Allen and Roswell argue, "changes the essential meaning of writing assessment from the assessment of writing to the assessment of writers" (1989, p. 11).

These short papers furnish teachers with immediate information they can use to plan the next quarter, the next week, or even the next day. At the same time, students have an opportunity to regularly describe and reflect on their own learning, reinforcing the learning as it is made conscious.

SSEs Focusing on Work Spanning Several Weeks. As the focus of the SSE widens and students describe learning over a longer period of time, the SSE usually also grows in length.

At Washington State University, two faculty members in architecture ask each student to keep a "design journal" associated with their design classes. The faculty want students to become conscientious about keeping a continuous record of their thinking and design processes, to build the habit of "drawing what you cannot write, and writing what you cannot draw." Realizing that the process of recording design ideas in a journal is new to most students, the faculty ask students to comment periodically on the development of their journals, to state what would help them develop as journal keepers, and to declare how they might improve their journal work. Students respond to these questions in short, in-class SSEs, which the faculty members call "five-minute writes" or "fifteen-minute writes." Three weeks into the course, one architecture student commented on her journal work,

> I need to write more details and descriptions of my work, telling how I chose what I did, analytically as well as graphically, . . . analyze my notes a little more, how I feel about certain things discussed in class and my interpretations of the design concept being studied, . . . more descriptions of the processes. [Five-minute write, architecture student, Washington State University]

Another developed a list of activities to work on:

> Need to put *more* descriptive details and processes; I failed to put enough process into the product. Put in more experiences that affect me through the day. Be more creative with format and design. Always improve. [Five-minute write, architecture student, Washington State University]

A "fifteen-minute write" on design journals later in the term may reveal student development related to the reflective work in design. This student struggled on paper with the idea of writing down his reflections on his work:

> The problem I have is that it's hard for me to write down the design process. Personally I don't want to call this a problem, because I believe the most amount of energy we need to put into the design process is the first part of the process: think, rethink, rethink the idea. I can hardly write this down in a journal. But in order to show teachers what I did, I have to be able to write this down. I am trying very hard to do this. [Fifteen-minute write, architecture student, Washington State University]

Even in the context of these short exercises, students often reflect on and make a commitment to future plans for their work:

Up until this point, I feel that I have been able to aptly grasp the concepts and ideas presented in this class and been able to apply it to each successive project and each stage within the projects. As far as being able to express this comprehension in the form of a journal, the accomplishment is somewhat near mediocrity. I understood what should be contained in the journal but started off slow and have been gaining speed ever since. My journal should exemplify my increased understanding from class to class and show a steady progression in a positive direction. [Five-minute write, architecture student, Washington State University]

Similarly, in an upper-division "Physical Systems" program at The Evergreen State College, faculty members want students to reflect on their work in collaborative problem solving. After a series of two-hour workshop sessions involving problems in the mathematical behavior of chaotic systems, a teacher asked students to spend a half hour writing specifically on what they had learned about their learning. One student focused on her collaborative work:

I worked with Adam for most of this workshop. Today Michael joined us in our endeavor. There was a big difference for me between working with one other person and working with two others. When two of us worked together we stayed together. We were always working on the same problem at the same time. If one of us didn't understand something, neither of us moved on until it was clear. When three of us got together, we all seemed to be doing different things. Someone always seemed to be way ahead or way behind, with intense intervals when we tried to explain things to each other. [Informal SSE, "Physical Systems" student, The Evergreen State College]

Another examined her approach to problem solving:

I can design a beadwork tapestry in my head, then go home and work out the particulars on paper. I do it all the time. The mind-set it takes to translate a chunk of old architecture or a wrought-iron fence into a twisty panel of beads is *exactly* the same one you use to manipulate bars of imaginary bread dough. That bread dough folding part was easy and vivid. Thinking about it algorithmically was less pleasant. "Seeing a pattern and manipulating it" is *not* the same as "seeing a pattern, turning it into an equation, and manipulating the equation." Attaching the equations to pictures often struck me as redundant, and tended to slow me down. I could often see the construct or the pattern perfectly well, but had to struggle for a few minutes to attach digits to the damned thing. [Informal SSE, "Physical Systems" student, The Evergreen State College]

In these cases, self-evaluation offers students an opportunity to view and examine their learning processes. Schmeck argues that students should "engage in deep and elaborative activities . . . to counteract the less desirable effects of a shallow-reiterative learning style" (1981, p. 385). These retrospective self-evaluation exercises do just that by asking students to do more than repeat the process. Writing an SSE gives students a chance to make it mean something.

SSEs Focusing on an Entire Course. These shorter excursions begin to chart the territory of self-evaluation in learning, an area most students have seldom entered. However, larger explorations occur when faculty ask students to write an SSE at the end of a course that reflects on what they have learned in the class and to what end. These SSEs, encompassing many weeks of study, are usually more formal and longer documents, often several typewritten pages.

Within these longer documents, seemingly simple discoveries may appear, but they are important discoveries, especially for a beginning student. At the conclusion of a Biology 101 course at Yakima Valley Community College, a freshman student wrote,

> One thing that I have really learned from this Biology class is the way to take tests. In taking tests, I have found that I must be more specific and thorough with my explanations. Being brief and vague doesn't help you learn anything, nor does it clarify your explanation for the reader of the test. So how can your instructor be sure that you have actually learned something if you can't clearly explain a process or answer a question? [Biology student, Yakima Valley Community College]

These documents again provide a formal occasion, perhaps the only one for students to describe difficulty and confusion from their own perspective. In a business law class at Lower Columbia College (Longview, Washington), a student focused a page of an SSE on critical thinking and writing about situations involving law:

> I've had to work very hard at critical thinking in this class. In real-life situations, I feel that I do more analyzing to come to decisions but the situations that were presented in class were more confusing to me because I wasn't familiar with laws. In class I noticed that I was quick to come to a conclusion, but as you brought up more issues, I found myself switching sides. It's uncomfortable to find out that you don't know which side to take in a situation. It shows that people need to examine all sides of an issue, ask more questions, and research rules and regulations when it comes to legal issues concerning contracts (or anything).
>
> Writing skills seemed so much different here than in an English Composition class. In English, my pen flowed much more freely. In this class I found I would stumble over words, write things down and then scratch them out as I thought of new ideas or new solutions. Law can be very confusing. [Business law student, Lower Columbia College]

The SSE provides a place for students to understand the seriousness of the issues they are studying. The content of our courses is obviously important for us who have worked with the material for so long, but often its importance is left implicit, and we do not give students the opportunity to make it important for themselves. Just as the law student built ideas for himself about multiple perspectives, another student used the self-evaluation process to wrestle with problems of being right or wrong. At Centralia College (Washington), this student described difficulties he encountered in Philosophy 101:

> Before relating what I am proud of I will retract something I am not proud of. During our discussion of paternalism I said, "To me this (philosophy) is a pseudoscience." I have pondered why I may have said that, and if it is true. I have been heavily indoctrinated in the natural sciences, and I believe in the concrete truths of biology and chemistry. However, as I was reading in my chemistry text I came across a sentence that has caused me to reflect. It reads "remember mechanisms (upon which chemistry is based) can never be established with certainty, but represent only our best present explanations of experimental observations." What do we actually know to be true? Is one science greater than another? Perhaps only to the individual. Finally, the enduring strength of philosophy for me is that it asks the question, what are the implications of my actions. And if I attain any skill in my life the most important will be my ability to be just, empathetic, and responsible in my actions. [Philosophy student, Centralia College]

Discovering that one does not understand is a large part of college learning, but it is a discovery that unfortunately can be interpreted, especially by a student, as "failure." Self-evaluation allows the student to use that "failure" as a place to begin to learn. At the conclusion of the previously mentioned architecture class, a student looked at the overall process of the design journal in an extensive SSE. This student shifted the focus of the way he handled the assignment and created a genuine "aha" for himself:

> I can see now that I wasn't using the journal as a design tool, but rather designing the journal. . . . I was able to use the journal portion for the previous projects as a reference . . . , but still I wasn't using the journal properly. As I read a lot of my notes and comments throughout the journal I noticed a drastic improvement in that I moved from simply spitting up what was presented in class to have some of my original thoughts and ideas and *recording* these thoughts. Those are the parts of my journal I cherish the most. [End-of-semester SSE, architecture student, Washington State University]

At Fairhaven College, an interdisciplinary undergraduate college within a larger regional university (Western Washington University), students write SSEs at the end of every course—often to synthesize the material learned in class. For a junior-level course, "Politics of Language," a student wrote,

These activities gave me the opportunity to articulate my understanding of the material covered in the book. I did this specifically by writing a paper called "The Impact of the Reagan Budget on Women," in which I applied some of Edelman's ideas to a critique of President Reagan's State-of-the-Union Address. In my paper I demonstrated how the rhetoric of President Reagan contradicts his policies toward women (as outlined by the Coalition on Women and the Budget composed of 66 women's education, religious, and labor organizations). ["Politics of Language" student, Fairhaven College, Western Washington University]

This essay included some application of critical thinking, but an SSE can also focus on reflection and candor. For a senior-level class, "Psycho-History," a student wrote,

Some two weeks ago, a friend picked up the standard text I was carrying around and asked what it was all about. He's in honors, applying to graduate schools, and I was surprised by the question.

"It's for an independent study I'm doing in Psycho-History," I said. "Just finishing up."

"Psycho-History?" he asked. "What's that?"

I briefly explained the topic as best I could (as well as the purpose of the hyphen in separating the "psycho" from the "history"), and though I stumbled over what I said, I secretly prided myself on having something to say at all.

There's not much to say about my exam. I got a "C".

I've written one (5 page) essay and read over 700 pages of material—Erikson, Barzun, Gay, selections from Febvere and Runyan—but I haven't found the time to read current articles or to give Barzun a thorough going-over. I read only two chapters in Stannard—the introduction and the conclusion. It's been a precipitate and superficial preface to an important branch of history.

I've bitten off a ridiculous amount of work this quarter, and my performance in this contract shows the futility of overstressing myself. Never again. ["Psycho-History" student, Fairhaven College, Western Washington University]

In English composition classes, many faculty ask students to write a self-reflective essay about ways their writing has improved during the course or since entering college. This is usually the last assigned essay in the class. An element of the essay usually involves the student's future plans for writing. Faculty encourage students to move beyond simply listing their skills with various mechanics of writing to reflecting on their relationship to writing. Students' ability to shift focus often depends on how much time was spent on self-evaluation in the course and how comfortable students feel about discussing their attitudes toward the writing process. The shift in focus to the student's relationship to the discipline may also be a function of the "prompt" or question in an assignment, in response to which a student develops insights about her own learning process. A woman whose first language was Amharic wrote,

> When I wrote my second essay, which was about the personal and cultural experiences I had in Ethiopia, I began to feel angry. . . . I wanted to shout while I was writing. I wanted the words I was writing to have a voice, to shout as loud as I would if I was speaking. . . . I wanted to say something through the essay. I wanted to make sense instead of counting the words and wondering if it met the amount of words our teacher told us to write. I was conscious of what I was doing; it was like I was speaking.

She concluded,

> Writing is not a pain anymore; it is something to enjoy. It is not a burden; it is a relief, a means of taking the inside feelings out. For me, writing is not just a class anymore, it is a means of developing power in my voice. [English composition student, Seattle Central Community College]

The final self-evaluation assignment, then, can provide the student with a location from which to perceive and articulate her own changing relationship to the craft and art of writing. The SSE at the end of a course can help students make the course something more whole and more meaningful for themselves. Students may also begin to construct themes on which to plan learning for the future.

SSEs Encompassing More Than a Single Course. When the focus of student self-evaluation shifts to include learning in more than a single class, not only does the scope change, but the process often does as well.

Student self-evaluation is a staple of many learning community curricula. *Learning community* refers to classes clustered around an interdisciplinary theme that enroll a common group of students. This restructuring of traditional courses gives students more coherence in their learning and gives students and teachers together a greater sense of academic community (Gabelnick, MacGregor, Matthews, and Smith, 1990). At present, dozens of learning community programs exist at colleges and universities around the country. They vary from two linked courses to complex coordinated studies programs in which both students and teachers are engaged full time. However, all programs involve students in constructing meaning together with their teachers and in building connections and comparisons between ideas and disciplines. At the end of the term, the self-evaluation process becomes the occasion for students to pull together themes and elements of their studies and to develop a written synthesis of their learning.

The University of Washington has pioneered an interdisciplinary writing program, a linked-course, learning community model that involves several hundred students each year. Intensive writing courses are linked to content courses in the general education curriculum at the university. Cohorts of students in each writing course are also enrolled in one of fifteen general education courses; the work in the writing course draws on both the questions and the mode of discourse in the linked course. In some of these linked writing classes, an end-of-term assignment asks students to assemble a portfolio of writing organized by a reflective essay; one assignment for such an essay is included in the appendix. Students prepare for this assignment throughout the quarter by "answering questions about their writing, reflecting on each other's writing, and characterizing their own writing and writing processes in terms of what they see each other doing" (Johnson-Bogart, 1992, p. 1). One student began the reflective essay with this paragraph:

> Analysis of these pieces has opened my eyes to the fact that I have become much more adept at intertwining critical thinking, the use of previous and newly acquired knowledge, and an incorporation of a geographic mind-set to effectively present my research and ideas on paper. My writing process as presented in these pieces has shown a direct link between thinking, writing, and reading. At each stage I have thought out how I could present something more effectively, what relevance or place my own critical analysis and/or research had with the problem and solutions I was trying to present, and what I could learn from a critique of other people's writing. I also was constantly reading, whether it was going through an article for the fifth time trying to find that critical piece of evidence or skimming through one of my drafts again to look for places it did not flow very well. . . . These ideas have been rather general so far, but I feel they will become clearer as I discuss each piece I have included in my portfolio. [Final essay, Interdisciplinary Writing Program student, University of Washington]

Faculty members do not see the SSE assignment at the end of the term as an "add-on." Continuous reflective work and the frequent sharing of writing through peer writing groups helps students develop a critical stance toward their writing throughout the term. The portfolio work gives faculty "an opportunity to see inside individual students, to see how they think about writing and learning and how they see themselves as participants in this process in general and in a particular disciplinary discourse. These are meta-issues that ground and inform the form and content of what students write, but which often remain invisible because they are not consciously addressed by students in their writing" (Johnson-Bogart, 1992, p. 2).

Student self-evaluation also plays a prominent role in coordinated studies, a more ambitious learning community model that comprises all the students' work during a given term. These programs of team-taught interdisciplinary study have a long history in U.S. higher education, going back to Meiklejohn's

Experimental College at the University of Wisconsin in the 1920s. In 1970, The Evergreen State College was established with coordinated studies as its primary curricular structure, and Evergreen continues with it today. In the past decade, other colleges have launched coordinated studies programs as an alternative general education pathway. These team-taught programs address interdisciplinary questions or themes, such as "The Televised Mind," "American Dreams, Lost and Found," "Speaking for Ourselves: The African American Experience," "Disease as Metaphor and Reality," and "The Paradox of Progress." Coordinated studies are not a cluster of separate classes but rather a new community relying on a variety of disciplines and connections to address the program's theme. At the end of the program, and often midway through, SSEs and faculty evaluations of students are exchanged and discussed in an individual conference between faculty and student.

In these more comprehensive learning communities, students are challenged to look back on an entire term's work, or in some cases an entire year's work, and to bring a synthesis to the experience in an essay.

As the student grows better acquainted with the process, the product often changes. Students writing their first SSE may take time to write about study skills and their relation to learning:

> Although not adequately prepared mathematically for the "Matter and Motion" curriculum, I feel I have made a great deal of progress this quarter in both physics and chemistry. I was able to compensate somewhat for my inadequate background by finding a math tutor to help me with geometry and trigonometry while at the same time I attempted to keep up with class. ["Matter and Motion" student, The Evergreen State College]

A beginning student may describe learning as a listing of work completed:

> I have developed a considerable degree of self-discipline this year. I learned to structure time efficiently and have come to take reading assignments in stride that were overwhelming at first. In fall quarter, for instance, we read eighty percent of the Old Testament and I had difficulty keeping up. By the time winter quarter reading assignments like Milton's *Paradise Lost* and *Last Days of Socrates* came up, however, I was sufficiently organized to complete them without undue stress and was able to enjoy them as well. [Core program student, The Evergreen State College]

Three years later, in a coordinated studies program on psychological counseling, this student wrote a much more reflective essay, describing connections she had made between books in the field and consulting she had done with "three psychologists concerning behavioral and psychological difficulties arising from problems experienced by learning disabled children." In her self-evaluation, she applied her learning to a particular context:

These materials and the meetings impressed me with the importance of flexibility and sensitivity to the uniqueness of the individual and his specific
problems and experiences as a prerequisite to successful therapy. These factors, I came to see, are more essential than any particular technique. In fact,
loyalty to any one therapeutic technique to the exclusion of all others can
be more harmful than helpful if it interferes with the therapist's ability to
recognize and honor the individuality of the client. [Psychological counseling student, The Evergreen State College]

In SSEs, somewhere between enumerating topics with little or no connections and applying the learned knowledge and processes to a particular
plan or context, is a step in which the student synthesizes what has been
learned:

Through the years of reading I have come to realize that it is a common trait
of mankind to rationalize action by forming a code of behavior. In particular Max Weber's *The Protestant Ethic and the Spirit of Capitalism* taught me to
view the "great questions" from a standpoint of totality—taking all factors
into account and not giving precedence to any one over others. Ellison's *The
Invisible Man* illustrated to me the need for each individual to gain his own
identity by acting in accordance with [his] own beliefs and not those of society—though the laws of society cannot and must not be avoided. ["Paradox
of Progress" student, The Evergreen State College]

Students frequently move from listing their experiences to defining their
new relationship with the course content:

I learned a lot about writing skills from the literature that I read. This
amounted to six books: *Obasan* by Joy Kagawa, *America Is in the Heart* by
Carlos Bulosan, *Silences* by Tillie Olsen, *At a Journal Workshop* by Ira Progoff,
The Bone People by Keri Hulme, and *Betsey Brown* by Ntozake Shange. Of
these (four fiction and two theoretical) books, I was most inspired by Joy
Kogawa and Keri Hulme as to written style. Both authors move easily from
writing in the narrative style to the dream or metaphorical sphere, and are
equally proficient at both. This is a style I would like to emulate, and
towards which direction my own work naturally leans. [Cross-cultural com-
munications student, The Evergreen State College]

These examples indicate that students progress through different skills
while writing SSEs. Initial attempts often begin with a plan for learning and a
naming or listing of topics and activities in the course or program. Later, with
practice, the writing develops in complexity to support a synthesis of learning
and a description of one's relationship to the learning. SSEs may eventually
include connections to other academic work or personal goals and a more

substantive evaluation of learning. (For a penetrating examination of the writing done in student self-evaluation, see Thompson, 1992.)

Classes Emphasizing Student Self-Reflection. Interest in the value of student self-evaluation has developed enough in Washington State to create both entry-level and capstone courses focused on self-evaluation.

Entry-level courses at Antioch University, Seattle, and at Seattle Central Community College ask students to construct an autobiography of themselves as learners. At Antioch, this required experience is called the "Art of Learning." At Seattle Central, the course is an elective. A required capstone seminar at Western Washington University's Fairhaven College asks students to write a Summary and Evaluation paper about their undergraduate career.

Several of the faculty members at Seattle Central Community College were feeling frustrated because student self-evaluation, which seemed to work so well in eighteen-credit interdisciplinary programs, was not always so successful in separate standing courses. The SSEs seemed less complex and often did not go beyond the "descriptive lists" level. At the same time, the college's Outcomes Task Force was searching for ways other than standardized testing to gain a view of student learning at the school. To serve our own purposes and those of the students, as well as the larger institution, we developed a standing course in self-evaluation entitled "Ways of Knowing." It is a five-credit, 100-level, writing-intensive humanities elective (HUM 150).

Through the first part of the quarter, students examine their educational goals as well as learning styles, developmental or stage theories of learning, cultural and philosophical definitions of learning, and obstacles to learning. In their reading they examine what "knowing" is from philosophical and psychological perspectives, as in *Women's Ways of Knowing* (Belenky, Clinchy, Goldberger, and Tarule, 1986) and Plato's *Meno*. A few different instruments—such as the Myers-Briggs Type Indicator, Kolb's Learning Style Inventory, and Witkin's Group Embedded Figures Test—introduce students to concepts of learning styles. We agree with Claxton and Murrell (1987) in their assertion that the Myers-Briggs Type Indicator is an effective way to begin a conversation with students about how they learn. By writing about and discussing their results on such tests, students begin to view themselves as learners, many for the first time.

At midterm, students write a profile of themselves as learners—which includes their roles with family, friends, and co-workers—and examine their prior learning experiences in schools. This autobiographical profile helps students gain a place for themselves in the college. College often seems alien and formidable to beginning students, especially first-generation college students. As Vincent Tinto points out in *Leaving College* (1987), unless the student finds a place in a new cultural setting and feels connected to it, he or she will often "give up" and leave that culture. At Seattle Central Community College, the autobiographical essay in the "Ways of Knowing" course seems to give students a place to tell their own story and be given credit for it in a new cultural setting. We have repeatedly seen that this validation assists students with finding and describing a niche or place in college.

Throughout the "Ways of Knowing" course, students keep a "journal of learning." In it they focus on what they are learning in the class and on what they are learning from week to week in the other classes in which they are enrolled. In the final essay, students write an SSE in which they match the self-portraits of themselves written during the first half of the quarter with the learning process in their concurrent classes and learning at the college.

The effect of the course on students is immediate. They often grow enthusiastic about having the time to explore in detail what learning is and to reflect on what they are currently learning and why. Reasons to study the material, implicit in the curriculum, are made explicit by the students. A different kind of conversation is created about what is happening in college. The SSEs look quite a bit like those already excerpted here, but the course allows more time for students to explore issues of confidence, motivation, and commitment. These issues emerge regularly, allowing students to demonstrate what is often not shown in more typical courses—a breakthrough understanding of what learning is about:

> My ideas about learning have changed this quarter in that I HAVE IDEAS ABOUT LEARNING. Up until this quarter I had never really focused on this, as an idea. Through "Ways of Knowing" I have given much finely tuned focusing to the way I learn and it has been useful (though painfully difficult at times). It has broadened my perspective and allowed me to hear more. I have been so used to seeing things MY WAY for so long, there has been no need for me to change very much (except maybe in areas of relationships). I have held on to my concepts and values tenaciously. Though I don't intend to let them go completely, I am more open to new and revised ideas. [Final paper, "Ways of Knowing" student, Seattle Central Community College]

The "Ways of Knowing" course explicitly makes students responsible for their own learning. Because the locus of control is explicitly placed with students, they are usually remarkably responsive and excited. When given the opportunity, students are eager to connect their learning to their world. In the same way, teaching the importance of lifelong learning becomes part of the process of education:

> Both subjects I took this quarter helped me grow internally. I learned more facts in Environmental Science, but these facts led to new internal convictions. . . . Ways of Knowing helped me examine barriers I've placed on myself in the past, and possible blocks I'll have in the future. But the strand that makes them both so similar is the new light of ideas that has been turned on. Thoughts are the things that inspire and challenge us to learn and be more, always exploring what we believe to be real. [Final paper, "Ways of Knowing" student, Seattle Central Community College]

The "Ways of Knowing" course focuses on approaches to learning and asks students to apply that content by reflecting carefully on who they are as learners and what is expected of them in a college setting. Students report that taking the course and writing the SSEs help them arrive at concepts both about learning and about their learning. At the same time, SSEs from the course have been used by the college to assess outcomes; this work is discussed in Chapter Five. "Ways of Knowing" at Seattle Central Community College has attracted national and international attention as a highly enriched freshman seminar or "University 101" experience.

Capstone courses also offer fruitful occasions for student self-evaluation. In addition to writing regular end-of-course SSEs, all students at Fairhaven College at Western Washington University must take a capstone seminar at the end of their undergraduate career. In this writing-intensive advanced seminar, students examine their entire college career in a formal Summary and Evaluation paper. In this paper, students describe and critically evaluate their experience in college. They pay attention both to ways in which the institution helped or hindered their progress and to their own developing knowledge of their subject matter and themselves as learners. The Summary and Evaluation paper requires students to take a self-evaluative stance as they reflect back not just on a course but on their entire college experience. The paper and the faculty member's written response to it become part of the student's permanent portfolio at the college. The senior seminar and the paper together are usually a rewarding experience for students (Eaton, 1992):

> The Advanced Seminar is one of Fairhaven's meaningful rituals, making graduating a meaningful experience. I was obsessed for weeks by the process of summing up and evaluating my entire, lifelong education. [Summary and Evaluation paper, Fairhaven College, Western Washington University]

In the senior seminar, faculty members frequently use a series of readings, activities, and prompting questions to help students identify themes they might want to develop more in their final paper. (An example of a prompt is provided in the appendix.) Students then work through a series of drafts of their Summary and Evaluation papers, with feedback from faculty and other students. The idea is not to present a litany of all the classes taken but to discuss how the classes and their themes were related, how a particular line of interest or questioning was followed, and what stood out as important. As one student put it in her Summary and Evaluation paper,

> The seminar has provided a wonderful structure within which I have been able to thoughtfully look back over my four years, reviewing, questioning, bringing to articulation a portrait in words of my experience here. . . . Writing my "Summary and Evaluation" was a chance for me to come to a sense of completion with what I have accomplished at Fairhaven College and to also see I take with me much work still to be done.

[Summary and Evaluation paper, Fairhaven College, Western Washington University]

An example of a complete Summary and Evaluation paper from Fairhaven College is provided in the appendix.

Capstone experiences like these go far in helping students to find strands of meaning in their college experience, to identify and describe coherent themes, to discuss intellectual discoveries or personal changes, and to consider a college education in the context of one's next step in life. As graduation day approaches, students naturally look backward and ahead. This kind of capstone experience creates time and space in the curriculum—real time and space—so that reflection not only occurs but also becomes explicit and can be responded to by fellow students and by teachers.

The SSE Assignment

Because SSEs are used in so many different settings, naturally students can be asked to write them in a variety of ways. The "prompt," or the way the teacher frames the SSE assignment, is at least partially governed by what the teacher wants students to examine and to learn in their writing. However, an SSE, unlike many other assignments, has no correct answer. To play off the title of Raymond Carver's short story, what we ask when we ask what someone has learned becomes complicated.

As may be expected, no ideal "generic assignment" has been created for student self-evaluation—and probably shouldn't be. The appendix of this volume provides examples of a variety of assignments or "prompts." Generally, SSE assignments range from quite specific questions to general ones. At one extreme are cut-and-dried questions about learning: "Did your knowledge of calculus improve this semester?" "Are you a better writer now than you were in September?" These kinds of questions naturally push the student into a "yes-or-no" kind of box. They usually produce very limited and superficial responses. At the other extreme are open-ended questions: "You have been on a quest this quarter for something and now you have found it—what is it?" These questions steer students away from producing what they feel is a prescribed answer or trying to second-guess what the teacher wants. Assignments that are too open-ended (like this example, perhaps) may produce high anxiety among many students and may frustrate faculty. The best prompts are therefore probably somewhere between the two extremes.

SSE prompts also differ in the kind of stance they expect students to take in their writing. Many SSE assignments ask students to take an analytical approach and to steer clear of "evocative," personal, or emotional material or emphases. Similarly, in professional fields such as social work, nursing, and education, many teachers create SSE assignments that explicitly request students to evaluate their professional development in courses or practica and to avoid addressing issues of personal development. However, some faculty prefer a more "personal" or "connected" approach to SSEs, so that students can not only make the material and their work with it important for their planned profession but also put it in the context of their personal lives and values. In either case, students are claiming their work in their own words. However, as will be discussed in the next chapter, teachers who prefer a more personal, connected approach must honor the boundaries of disclosure that students set for themselves.

In all cases, the goal of student self-evaluation is for students to assume responsibility for describing what they have learned and what they plan to do with it. Students who have become more aware of their own thinking can better meet that challenge. When designing prompts, faculty members must keep in mind their own objectives for the assignment while handing students the responsibility for describing their learning.

Grading and Feedback

Should SSEs be graded or not? If they are not graded, will students take them seriously? Our colleagues continuously struggle with these questions. The answers, like the faculty and institutions from which they come, are diverse; like the choices of prompts they are also linked to context. Whether they grade SSEs or do not, teachers often have strong opinions about their particular approach.

Some faculty ask for SSEs as regular formal assignments that are given grades—especially when students are writing SSEs to describe the portfolio of work that they present at the end of a course. Some teachers have created rubrics with which to grade SSEs. Other teachers are adamant about never grading SSEs, and they take the time to give students careful and detailed feedback either in writing or through conferences with each student. Some faculty members may not grade the SSEs but still use them as an indicator of what a student has learned when determining the student's final grade for a class. Many faculty ask for SSEs at the end of the term but do not read or respond to them until after all grades are turned in.

Grading SSEs may bring students back to the game of guessing what the teacher wants to read or putting what they hope will be the best "spin" on their work. Some faculty argue that grading SSEs thus defeats nearly all the purposes of student self-evaluation. Many teachers who do assign and give grades on SSEs say that grading an SSE is similar to grading a painting, a short story, a poem, or given the context of a particular assignment from a particular class, a reflective essay. When evaluating any of these products for a class, faculty have explicit or implicit criteria for what is "good work." If a grade is offered, the written or oral feedback that accompanies the grade is crucial. Students deeply appreciate teachers' responses that are detailed and constructive.

Whether or not the SSE is graded, the important question is what response to an SSE is appropriate. The student's SSE must be taken seriously, and its consideration needs to become a formal part of the student's educational experience. Students take SSEs seriously to the degree that faculty members take them seriously. SSEs seem to work most successfully when self-reflection is interwoven throughout the course rather than tacked on at the end.

Conclusion

Whether they use SSEs in modest or ambitious ways, teachers who integrate self-evaluation into their classes become more intentional about teaching the skills of self-evaluation and responding to the SSEs that students write. Teachers provide students with tangible experiences to build self-evaluation writing skills, with such activities as handing out major SSE assignments early in the course; sprinkling short, reflective SSE work throughout the course; providing examples (not models) of SSEs; facilitating collaborative composing sessions with small groups; or assigning a learning journal so that students will have material from which to draw directly when they write. However, if the structural supports are too rigid, they could imply for students a predesignated response and hamper the value and quality of student-originated work. Learning environments in which students synthesize, explore, and create on their own, interacting with the material with others, are ultimately the most conducive to meaningful student self-evaluation.

References

Allen, M. S., and Roswell, B. S. "Self-Evaluation as Holistic Assessment." Paper presented at the annual meeting of the Conference on College Composition and Communication, Seattle, Wash., Mar. 1989. (ED 303 809)

Angelo, T. A., and Cross, K. P. *Classroom Assessment Techniques: A Handbook for College Teachers.* (2nd ed.) San Francisco: Jossey-Bass, 1993.

Belenky, M. F., Clinchy, B. M., Goldberger, N. R., and Tarule, J. M. *Women's Ways of Knowing: The Development of Self, Voice, and Mind.* New York: Basic Books, 1986.

Claxton, C. S., and Murrell, P. H. *Learning Styles: Implications for Improving Educational Practices.* ASHE-ERIC Higher Education Report, no. 4. Washington, D.C.: Association for the Study of Higher Education, 1987.

Eaton, M. D. "Student Self-Assessment: Thinking About the Way We Know." *Proceedings of the 10th Annual Conference on Nontraditional/Interdisciplinary Programs.* Fairfax, Va.: Center for Professional Development, George Mason University, 1992, pp. 55–69.

Gabelnick, F., MacGregor, J., Matthews, R., and Smith, B. L. *Learning Communities: Creating Connections Among Students, Faculty, and Disciplines.* New Directions for Teaching and Learning, no. 41. San Francisco: Jossey-Bass, 1990.

Johnson-Bogart, K. "Writing Portfolios: The Benefits for Teachers of Using Student Self-Assessment." Paper presented at the Washington State-Wide Assessment Conference, Spokane, Wash., May 1992.

Schmeck, R. "Improving Learning by Improving Thinking." *Educational Leadership,* 1981, 38, 384–385.

Taylor, K., and Marienau, C. "Self-Assessment: A Source for Individual and Organizational Learning." *Contemporary Education,* 1993, 64 (3), 166–169.

Thompson, K. *Learning at Evergreen (II): Writing and Thinking.* Report of the Assessment Study Group. Olympia, Wash.: Office of Research and Planning, Evergreen State College, 1992.

Tinto, V. *Leaving College: Rethinking the Causes and Cures of Student Attrition.* Chicago: University of Chicago Press, 1987.

CARL J. WALUCONIS is professor of English and humanities at Seattle Central Community College, Washington.

At first, self-evaluation is unfamiliar and challenging to most students. Teachers can use a variety of approaches to support students in their first attempts at self-evaluation writing.

Learning Self-Evaluation: Challenges for Students

Jean MacGregor

Those of us who have involved students in writing and talking about their self-evaluations know how illuminating the process is to us and to them. In thinking carefully and writing about their work, many of our students build confidence and develop a sense of responsibility as learners. Many get inklings of what it means to probe more deeply into their learning and thinking. Many begin to view specific learning experiences against the broader terrain of their undergraduate experience. Some students use these occasions to identify new directions or goals for their learning. Others describe new connections or venture hunches about academic ideas.

Although we often see sparks of curiosity and insight in student writing, not all students make these leaps, nor do all students find self-evaluation useful or illuminating—at least not at first. Almost always, writing student self-evaluations for the first time is a strange experience, and students may greet the process with confusion, anxiety, or suspicion.

This chapter describes some of the challenges students face as they learn to write SSEs and suggests some ways we can respond to them. These observations have grown out of my experiences using student self-evaluation in my own teaching, reading myriad SSEs, and talking with both faculty colleagues and, more importantly, students about the self-evaluation process.

Challenges for Students

Our students generally come to us well adjusted to (if not highly successful in) educational settings that do not, as a rule, cultivate learners as central agents in their own learning and knowing. Most beginning students come to college expecting to accumulate—or in Paulo Freire's (1970) term, "bank"—knowledge given to them by textbooks and teachers. They expect to be ranked on knowledge they receive and accurately reproduce for tests. In this game of "banking" and "ranking," most students accept that it is the teacher's purview to make judgments about what is important to learn and what learning is important to assess. As William Perry's study (1970) and the *Women's Ways of Knowing* study (Belenky, Clinchy, Goldberger, and Tarule, 1986) point out, these students have yet to develop the intimate connections between knowers and knowledge, between learners and learning. A task that asks them to write reflectively and subjectively about these connections is understandably foreign and demanding.

Unfamiliarity with Looking Inward at Learning. Self-examination outside the realm of academia is not new to students; they undoubtedly give much critical thought to their looks and the clothes they wear, the way they dance or play a sport. But sustained reflection on their learning processes is generally unfamiliar. Students have little experience examining their academic work in any systematic way and even less experience describing it in writing. Years of schooling have conditioned them to think of evaluation as a series of discrete episodes in which they produce work for the teacher to grade. Any evaluating the student does is evaluating the teacher and the course, often at its end, through questionnaires or survey instruments. Of course, students worry about doing well in classes, but more often they are concerned about the grade they will be "given," not about their mastery of the course material, the way that accomplishment relates to the rest of their academic program or their life plans, or the larger meanings they can draw from the experience.

Many beginners at self-evaluation omit the self and write about the teacher or the course, or they cloak their experience in such vague generalizations as this:

> I feel that I have gained a great deal of knowledge since enrolling in [Program X]. Many questions that I had before have now been answered. I feel that if I remain in the program (I intend to) I could become a highly knowledgeable individual about many things. [The Evergreen State College, quoted in Thompson, 1992, p. 33]

Lack of Confidence in Describing Their Own Learning. As teachers we frequently note how difficult it is for beginning students to articulate what they think, so accustomed are they to thinking or inferring what we want them to think or expect them to think. For those students who do not yet trust their own experience, ideas, or questions as having academic integrity or importance, it is a struggle, at first, to find something to say.

Many students stay in the safe territory of enumerating likes or dislikes but with little elaboration or analysis:

I was happy with all the books that had been included in the initial class list. Among my favorites were Angelou's *I Know Why the Caged Bird Sings,* and Miller's *The Crucible.* I was caught up in the reading of the two books, because they struck an emotional chord with me. Literature that moves me to be sad, happy, or angry, tends to pull a tougher argument from me. I found *all* the books to be completely useful and significant to the subjects and discussions at hand. The newspaper clippings and copies were excellent sources of information when writing journals and papers. [Student in business law class, Lower Columbia College]

Cataloguing the most useful or interesting elements of the course is typical of many beginning evaluations. Yet the sentence "Literature that moves me . . . tends to pull a tougher argument from me" is a tantalizing one, one I would ask the student to explain in a conference or to develop in a second draft of the SSE.

Other students are unclear about the purposes and audience for self-evaluation, like this architecture student who, as she was learning the process of keeping a design journal (a vehicle for ongoing self-evaluation) used her SSE to ask for direction from her faculty member:

I would like to know, am I writing to you? I know I write my thoughts down. I know what's going on, but do you? Is this design journal for me or for you? Do others need to know what's going on? [Five-minute, in-class self-evaluation of design journal work, architecture student, Washington State University]

Perhaps students simply need time to recognize that SSEs really are for them. At the end of her academic career, this student described this recognition:

I did not develop the mature attitude necessary for writing evaluations until my junior year when I realized evaluations should be written for me, not to convince the professor to give me a good report. The evaluation process benefited me so much in clearly defining my goals and interests that I wish I had written evaluations in graded classes to define for myself my experiences in them. [Summary and Evaluation, Fairhaven College, Western Washington University]

As we introduce self-evaluation to students and support them in their first attempts, we can encourage students to regard SSEs as ways not just to report to us on their learning experience but to describe it in their own words and indeed to "define it for themselves."

Problems with Writing. Beginning students may have not much to say in SSEs about their learning, and they may have trouble expressing what they do have to say. Writing anxiety may set in. Other students may not take the writing task seriously or bring to the task what they should know about organizing academic essays. Vague writing, collections of unconnected comments, or stiff and plodding prose, which communicate limited passion or engagement with learning, reveal students who are going through the motions for us.

Admittedly, most undergraduate students are novices at academic writing. Figuring out how to capture a learning experience that spans work over several weeks or a year—or, more challenging still, one's whole undergraduate career—may be a daunting task. In her Summary and Evaluation essay on her undergraduate experience, one student opened by describing the overwhelming nature of student self-evaluation.

> I sit in a heap of journals, evaluations, papers, notes, books, scripts, ditto sheets . . . proof of my college career . . . and I ask myself, "What does it all mean? What have I learned? How do I know what I know? How have I changed? What tools have I acquired, and how will they help me live my life? As an educated person, what responsibilities do I now have and to whom, and to what degree need I be responsible? How have my subjects of study affected my life as a woman? Where do I go from here?" [Summary and Evaluation, Fairhaven College, Western Washington University]

However, she then went on to answer these questions with remarkable depth and clarity.

The writing weaknesses that appear in SSEs are similar to those that appear in all undergraduate writing. Characteristically, SSEs suffer from seeing either the "forest" or the "trees." That is, students often generalize about their experience with little substantiation or exemplifying detail or enumerate particulars without drawing any larger synthesis or conclusion. We can point up these difficulties to students, particularly if we ask students to write short SSEs several times in a course or ask for a first draft on which we can give feedback.

Difficulty in Making Judgments About Their Work. As students become more comfortable with reflective writing, they start describing their process of learning and reporting on the compelling aspects of their experience. In addition, they may venture insights about the process or substance of their learning. However, most students are not sure how to evaluate their work—in the sense of appraising its worth, discussing its strengths or weaknesses, and articulating and supporting a judgment about the larger meaning or value of the learning experience. Alverno College's extensive studies of student self-assessment (1989) reveal that beginning students see evaluation as arbitrary and are not sure what criteria to use to examine their work or how to back up their perceptions with evidence. These studies and our own experience suggest that students generally remain uncertain of how to write evaluatively about themselves, particularly in the absence of explicit examples or criteria of successful work in the class or in the absence of occasions for systematically examining and reflecting on their work. Assessment cues and self-assessment practices can emerge from various activities: teachers' delineation of expected outcomes; frequent and constructive criticism of student work; frequent and ongoing reflective work by students in journals or short free-writing exercises; periodic examination or evaluation of student portfolios by students themselves, their peers, or their teacher; or frequent collaborative work among students in which they have the chance to hear, see, and respond to others' work.

Any one or combination of these activities can create an active interplay between work and reflection. But in the absence of the feedback that comes with frequent performance and response, students often write SSEs that steer clear of self-evaluation. Their writing is more a summation of work completed over the term or a narrative description of "how I learned" or "what worked well for me in the course":

> During Professor [X]'s class, there was a 50-50 communication exchange between the professor and the students, rather than the usual 100% lecture style where communication is only directed from the professor to the students. I found labs to be helpful in allowing us to view firsthand how the information we were learning applies to life. I found seminars to be helpful in showing us good communication skills to be applied not only in Biology. I found the fact that we concentrated only on one unit each week, and learning that subject inside and out to relieve a lot of the stress that can be accompanied with trying to absorb a large amount of material in a short period of time. Visual aids such as videotapes, videotaped slides, physical examples of molecules bonding (that you could touch) were all extremely helpful. [Biology student, Yakima Valley Community College]

If all students have is the faculty member's evaluation framework (either explicitly stated or implied), understandably students will begin by evaluating themselves within the boundaries of that framework. They lack a larger frame or vocabulary for describing other qualities of their learning and are not sure whether to venture beyond whatever boundaries are stated. Playing it safe, students often parrot back what teachers have set out as important. They write such phrases as "This course helped me learn to think critically" or "I learned to work toward more coherence in my writing," but they provide little or no evidence for these accomplishments.

Some students are quite explicit about their need for cues from the teacher, as was this junior-level student:

> It's difficult to write a self-evaluation this quarter without seeing [your] comments from the last three quizzes/examinations given during the last week of class. I don't think test-taking was my strongest area this quarter anyway, so I'm writing this with the assumption that the results of those quizzes were neutral. [Informal SSE, "Physical Systems" student, The Evergreen State College]

Critical examination of self is colored, of course, by the overall sense of self-esteem that each student brings to the task. Students new to self-evaluation and without a strongly developed sense of self may belittle their accomplishments or overblow them, again without specific evidence. Several recent studies in higher education show that undergraduate women consistently underestimate their abilities and that men generally overestimate theirs (Astin, Green, and Korn, 1987; Light, 1990). We are not aware of any studies that examine how self-esteem influences writing in SSEs or, conversely, how writing SSEs influences self-esteem, but this line of inquiry is worth pursuing.

Discomfort in Discussing Academic Difficulty. In conventional college classrooms, where the assumed game is to outcompete peers, students have become experts at masking their academic weaknesses or bluffing their way around them. Honestly admitting mistakes and shortcomings in an SSE can be an ordeal, particularly if students are unclear about whether a candid self-evaluation will lower their grade in the class. It takes some courage to expose vulnerabilities in paragraphs like these:

> There are still areas of my writing that frustrate me. I notice that I still have a tendency to repeat my ideas or words in the same paragraph. Another area I feel needs improvement is my sentence structure. I seem to stick to one style throughout my papers instead of varying it. These are parts of my writing that improved little. [Student in developmental English, Green River Community College]

> My speaking ability is practically invisible. I have always had a problem with speaking my thoughts on a subject. I have a very easy time holding a conversation among friends but once the atmosphere changes and it becomes a structured environment I clam up. I have never been able to speak in front of a group and I do not think I ever will be able to. I figured that if I was ever going to break myself of this bad fault, it would be through Integrated Studies. But I have failed there; if anything, Integrated Studies has made me close up even more. But even so, I have come to accept this fault of mine. [Integrated Studies student, University of North Dakota, quoted in Gabelnick, MacGregor, Matthews, and Smith, 1990, p. 73]

On the other hand, the self-evaluation process offers students the opportunity to face hurdles and to make breakthroughs:

> A big revelation came to me in writing seminar yesterday. We were asked to write a dialogue with our work. In the "conversation" I was having with my work, I discovered that I *hate* to be a beginner. I want to be an expert immediately, or not at all. This was a turning point for me, since I am an easy quitter. I've always wondered why I could never finish what I started, and why I couldn't make any of my projects turn out. . . . Last night, I thought of the

things I want to be good at and the things I want to study. I looked at myself in the mirror . . . and declared myself a novice. I felt a sense of relief, as I had been unburdened. [Student in "Looking at the Renaissance" coordinated studies program, Seattle Central Community College, quoted in Gabelnick, MacGregor, Matthews, and Smith, 1990, p. 72]

Cultural Discomfort with Self-Evaluation. Is student self-evaluation alien to some cultures? Is its use inappropriate with some groups of students? In both our own experience and that of the many colleagues of different cultural backgrounds with whom we have discussed this issue, we have not encountered evidence of a cultural bias against asking students to examine and discuss their work in SSEs. Nonetheless, in classrooms with a diversity of students, learning activities that we have come to take for granted may in fact provoke discomfort or confusion for some of our students. We wonder if, for those students whose upbringing and cultural experience value integral membership in a wider group or community, the act of calling attention to oneself in an SSE may be difficult. Claiming academic accomplishment, "tooting one's own horn," may seem like an inappropriate act of aggrandizement or individualism or simply bad manners. Sharing discoveries about one's learning or values with one's teacher may seem like improper revelation of confidences to a stranger. Some of our colleagues point out that, according to the norms of certain communities (some Native American communities, for example), the individual is not considered the right one to assess his or her own competence. If a person stands out, it is because the community recognizes the individual.

However, student self-evaluation can provide a unique platform for self-definition, for the claiming of one's own sense of self within the wider community of the class. In the "Ways of Knowing" class at Seattle Central Community College, a class built around reflecting on previous learning in school as well as learning in other classes (described in Chapter Two), a quarter to a third of the class typically is non-Caucasian, and many of these students are non-native English speakers. The teachers of these classes report that the students who enroll find the course personally illuminating and energizing. Many students remark that "Ways of Knowing" is the first class they have taken in which a teacher cared about who they are as learners and in which who they are as learners mattered to the entire agenda of the class. Differences among students frequently emerge, however, as students write their "autobiographies as learners," essays that reflect students' personal and political histories. Students from abroad are often struck by the apolitical and overly "psychologized" narratives of U.S. students. In turn, U.S. students are struck by the degree to which their non-American peers dwell on the political cauldrons that have shaped their learning and attitudes.

To what degree self-evaluation may impose on some students remains an open question. We suggest that faculty members always explicitly state their respect for student privacy in this kind of writing. If the SSE assignment is to be relatively open-ended, many teachers find it useful to provide a variety of prompting questions (as provided in the Appendix) so students can choose different writing emphases or perspectives.

Emotional Turbulence Beyond the Scope of the Academic Work. Although the act of reflecting itself may not confront cultural bias, the content of the reflection or the dynamics of the student-teacher relationship may trigger strong emotional responses. An African American colleague of ours recently described her work in self-evaluation as an undergraduate student. The racism she observed and experienced in her college classes triggered not only immediate rage but also old memories of personal humiliation. However, in the careful examination of those experiences she found a point of entry into academia and a desire to continue into a career in college teaching. At a conference on student self-evaluation, she related,

> I entered a process of writing to myself about my experiences in the institution, and in the classroom. The problem for me was learning to frame my experience in academic terms, and to understand what I thought about the content I was being introduced to. What I needed to write about was racism—beginning with the first day I set foot in grade school. And in college, I had to deal with racism in the content of the material we were using in various classes, content that I often found insulting and dehumanizing. I had to write about this in order to become authentic. I couldn't separate the content from what I was feeling about it. The way I had to write about it was not a way that I would want to show an employer or some one else. It took me probably a couple of years of writing about it in a "gunky" kind of way before I could get to the point where I could write much at all more for employers or an external audience. I fought all the way through about writing more objectively.
>
> As I look back now, the journal writing helped me to feel my way through my education. I realize now that I was also searching for my own epistemological roots while at the same time trying to understand something about the academic disciplines. [Personal communication, Jackie Moorey, Antioch University, Seattle]

This is just one instance of a student clarifying her work and her goals for her education through self-evaluation, but it is important to note that this writing was done in private at first. The fact remains that many students feel a gulf—a yawning gulf—between themselves and their teachers or between themselves and the subject matter of the class. When this distance is great or painful or humiliating, the student cannot help but ask, "How honest can I be in my SSE about what is really going on for me in this class? How vulnerable can I be?"

If reflecting on learning raises strong personal or emotional issues or challenges deeply held values or if students are experiencing turbulence in their lives outside class, students may struggle with deciding what and how much they should disclose in an SSE. Therefore, our SSE assignments should, and usually do, set boundaries for students as to what is appropriate. We need to make clear to students that we respect their privacy: Self-evaluation about learning in class should not be self-revelation in general. But we cannot predict the meanings our students will make of the course material or the emotional upheavals that are bound to occur in their lives.

As it was for our African American colleague, reflective writing can be a vehicle for examining and resolving personal issues. Self-evaluation often helps students clarify their emotional confusion, find solid ground, and move on in their lives. But not always. If our students risk honesty about emotional turmoil, we must listen and help them work constructively on whatever issues have been churned up. This support may involve encouraging them to do additional writing, to continue to talk with us, or in some cases to seek advice from the college's counseling staff. (For an excellent discussion of this issue, see Swartzlander, Pace, and Stamler, 1993.)

Confusion About Multiple Audiences and Purposes. Students generally write SSEs for their faculty member in a particular course or program. However, there can be other audiences for SSEs. SSEs may be written for academic advising purposes and become part of the student's file at the college. SSEs written for assessment purposes may be read by a wider group of faculty, administrators, or consultants. In some colleges or programs, SSEs are written to be included in the student's formal transcript. Any of these different uses may present beginning students with questions about audience and intentions in their writing.

Colleges like Antioch University, Seattle, and Goddard College have long required students to write end-of-term or end-of-year SSEs in preparation for meetings with a faculty adviser. More recently, some colleges have been linking student self-evaluations to advising programs that require portfolios of student work. Students write SSEs as progress reports to their adviser on all their course work and on their learning or degree goals. Beginning students, because they are not writing to an individual faculty member, often wonder whether to evaluate courses, teachers, themselves, or some combination. SSE assignments, such as the Quarterly Student Learning Assessment assignment, described in the appendix, can help focus student writing. So can the feedback that students receive in conferences about their SSEs with their faculty adviser.

In many assessment projects, SSEs are collected for assessment purposes only—for example, to evaluate the influence a learning community has on the intellectual development of students. Occasionally a formal SSE written during or at the end of a course is used by the teacher for both in-class purposes and assessment purposes. In either case, teachers generally ask students to sign consent forms permitting their SSEs to be reviewed by external readers, and students are aware of these audiences before they begin writing.

Even though assessment projects involving SSEs generally require that students write anonymously—at a minimum the SSEs are coded for scoring purposes so confidentiality is assured—in such circumstances, students may be reluctant to be as thorough and candid as they might otherwise be. In our experience, however, students generally take these SSE assignments seriously, especially if self-evaluation is a familiar classroom practice. One of the most critical factors in the student's willingness to be thoughtful and reflective in SSEs used for assessment purposes is the context set for them, usually by the faculty member in a classroom setting. The purpose of using SSEs for assessment is to gain a richer understanding of student learning, with the ultimate goal being to improve the overall educational quality of an institution. Faculty members who take the time to explain this purpose to students are usually rewarded with serious and thoughtful SSEs.

If faculty decide to require SSEs for formal inclusion in student transcripts (in study in a major or in a professional program, for example), additional questions about audience confront students. No longer are students writing an essay just to themselves and to their faculty member, but rather they are writing for a potential employer or a graduate school admissions officer. The anticipation of these more distant and judgmental audiences may give students a greater sense of consequence for their writing, and therefore the SSE assignment may be taken more seriously. Students may also be more cautious and more formal than they might otherwise be with their teacher or faculty adviser. Many students, feeling the pressure to "look good," write SSEs that catalogue accomplishments rather than reflect on learning. At colleges where SSEs are part of students' formal transcripts, such as The Evergreen State College, many faculty members ask students to write an "in-house" SSE to be discussed first and a second, more formal version for the transcript. Peter Elbow's suggestions for writing SSEs (included in the Appendix) address these questions of audience and explain the value of writing SSEs in two stages.

Suggestions for Teachers

These challenges for students are in turn challenges for us. Learning to write SSEs is like learning any new skill: The skill develops and deepens with practice and feedback. Chapter Four discusses more broadly the task of creating learning environments that foster self-evaluation, but here is a brief list of ways we can support students in their first attempts at student self-evaluation:

Set the context and rationale for ongoing reflective practice. Without some introduction, the self-evaluation process might be seen by students as just another hoop to jump through to get credit for the course. I introduce self-reflection as an essential capacity for meaningful learning and for living in a complex and paradoxical world. I acknowledge that organizing our reflective experiences and communicating them to others is demanding work and that self-evaluation skills improve with focused practice. Like many faculty members at Alverno College, I ask students to consider self-assessment in terms of one meaning for the word *assessment,* "sitting down beside." In self-evaluation writing, we are figuratively sitting down beside ourselves and gaining perspective on who we have been, who we are, and who we are becoming—as learners and knowers, as apprentices in a discipline, and as citizens in the world.

Integrate reflective work throughout the course. Self-evaluation generally is superficial and ineffective as a single episode at the end of the term. To develop as a habit or point of view about learning, self-evaluation should emerge as an ongoing process, through such course activities as learning journals, portfolio development, or "classroom assessment" strategies (Angelo and Cross, 1993). These need not be lengthy, time-consuming activities, nor do you need to read and respond to every piece of reflective work that students do. Like quick-sketching work in drawing classes, brief reflective writing at the end of a lecture, lab, or discussion session can develop observational power, writing fluency, and familiarity with the process.

Consider engaging students in collaborative learning. Through talking and listening to their peers, students clarify their ideas, become personally engaged with the course content, and get new perspectives on their own thinking. Involving students frequently in small-group work makes everyone's learning more public and gives students much more data to work with when they reflect on their own learning experiences.

Clarify the purposes and audience for more formal SSEs. As the examples of SSE assignments in both Chapter Two and the appendix demonstrate, the written products that teachers expect vary greatly. Some teachers have fixed protocols. Others, believing that SSEs should come entirely from the student, argue that the only appropriate prompt is to put before the student a blank page and the invitation to write. My experience is that too much ambiguity can overwhelm beginning students. It is useful to consider carefully what you want students to focus on and learn in the process and what you want to learn from them. And then give them a clear written assignment that explains how you plan to evaluate and respond to the SSE. How students shape their SSEs and what they tell you in them can provide ideas for developing and improving your SSE assignments.

Tailor responses to SSEs to support student development. Students repeatedly tell us that their teachers' encouragement, interest, and criticism help them build confidence and develop skill in writing SSEs. Asking students to write short SSEs and giving them timely feedback—whether through brief written responses or occasional conferences—can support students' first efforts and push them in longer SSEs to probe more deeply, clarify their insights, or further develop an idea. These occasional rituals of writing and feedback clarify for students whether their SSEs are meeting your expectations and how they might strengthen them.

What Students Have to Say

Ultimately, whatever students have to say in their SSEs—whether awkward or graceful, tentative or self-assured—is just that: what they have to say. That is the point. As we challenge and encourage students to write reflectively, they do in time gain confidence in describing what is working well for them, or what is important or difficult, and why. They identify what they are wondering about or worrying about or seeing with new eyes. They mention the connections they are making to the course material. They explore new plans or commitments that have grown out of their learning. When students write about things that are important to them and when we honor that writing, a special quality of community emerges that has to do with caring about learners and caring about learning.

References

Alverno College Assessment Council. "Self-Assessment: Summary Report." Milwaukee, Wis.: Alverno College Productions, 1989.

Angelo, T. A., and Cross, K. P. *Classroom Assessment Techniques: A Handbook for College Teachers.* (2nd ed.) San Francisco: Jossey-Bass, 1993.

Astin, A., Green, K. C., and Korn, W. S. *The American Freshman: Twenty-Year Trends 1966–85.* Los Angeles: Higher Education Research Institute, Graduate School of Education, University of California, 1987.

Belenky, M. F., Clinchy, B. M., Goldberger, N. R., and Tarule, J. M. *Women's Ways of Knowing: The Development of Self, Voice, and Mind.* New York: Basic Books, 1986.

Freire, P. *Pedagogy of the Oppressed.* New York: Continuum, 1970.

Gabelnick, F., MacGregor, J., Matthews, R., and Smith, B. L. *Learning Communities: Creating Connections Among Students, Faculty, and Disciplines.* New Directions in Teaching and Learning, no. 41. San Francisco: Jossey-Bass, 1990.

Light, R. *Explorations with Students and Faculty About Teaching, Learning, and Student Life.* Report of the Harvard Assessment Seminars, no. 1. Cambridge, Mass.: Graduate School of Education, Harvard University, 1990.

Perry, W. G. *Forms of Intellectual and Ethical Development in the College Years: A Scheme.* Troy, Mo.: Holt, Rinehart & Winston, 1970.

Swartzlander, S., Pace, D., and Stamler, V. L. "The Ethics of Requiring Students to Write About Their Personal Lives." *The Chronicle of Higher Education,* Feb. 17, 1993, pp. B1–B2.

Thompson, K. *Learning at Evergreen (II): Writing and Thinking.* Report of the Assessment Study Group. Olympia, Wash.: Office of Research and Planning, Evergreen State College, 1992.

JEAN MACGREGOR is associate director of the Washington Center for Improving the Quality of Undergraduate Education at The Evergreen State College.

The development and use of student self-evaluation is best supported
by specific educational and pedagogical frameworks.
These frameworks are in turn supported by
examples in the students' own voices.

Work, Reflection, and Community: Conditions That Support Writing Self-Evaluations

Marie Eaton, Rita Pougiales

In our teaching and work in institutions that use narrative self-evaluation as a central component in both student and faculty evaluation, we have read hundreds of student self-evaluations and have also written numerous self-evaluations of our own work. Writing SSEs is important in the learning experiences of our students and, we believe, in our teaching. In this chapter we reflect on the philosophical and pedagogical conditions that appear to support self-evaluation, share the observations of students who have incorporated SSEs into their academic experience, and discuss how student self-evaluation has affected us as teachers. We also discuss how the careful reflection required in reviewing and evaluating our own teaching has enabled us to make new connections and has deepened our understanding of the learning process. Reflection, a basic element of writing SSEs, causes us to look carefully and critically at our lives and work.

We share Pat Hutchings's view (1990) that college education should go beyond learning information specific to a discipline or major: "The object here is graduates who know their own strengths and weaknesses, can set and pursue goals, who monitor their own progress and learn from experience. There's considerable evidence now that students who are self-conscious about their processes as learners are better learners, that they learn more easily and deeply, and that their learning lasts. The fashionable label for the skills in question here is 'metacognitive,' but whatever you call them they represent a kind of learning that speaks to a belief that learning is personally liberating, self-empowering, and for all students" (p. 7). We believe that making SSEs a central part of the academic experience enhances and supports student development toward these objectives. In writing SSEs, students can accurately assess their own efforts, in addition to building a base from which they can improve future learning endeavors.

It is important to acknowledge the exercise of authority in higher education early in our discussion of SSEs. Underlying the extension of evaluation from faculty to students is a comparable extension of authority regarding the point of view and response to the academic material. By allowing for the possibility of individual engagement and articulation of response to the class content, the faculty transform academic authority from a singular exercise in evaluation to the shared work of the class.

Elements of Meaningful Student Self-Evaluation

In this chapter we will discuss three elements that provide the conditions for writing SSEs and that transform the experience of "schooling" into meaningful learning: the personalization of one's own work, reflection about that work, and the learning that takes place in a community. These conditions help make learning visible and relevant to students and teachers alike. These three conditions should not be separated. Although we are going to talk about them separately, they create a context and function together.

Work. In his discussion of pedagogy, Paulo Freire (1984) argues that students must be given "work" that they can own; the work must matter to them, not only because it draws on their experience but also because it allows them to better understand, and therefore change, their lives. The self-evaluation process can assist students to "perceive critically the way they exist in the world with which and in which they find themselves; [so they can] come to see the world not as a static reality, but as a reality in process, in transformation" (p. 71). Whether students' efforts are represented visually or in writing, some tangible product summarizing their work provides a substantive focus for reflection and criticism. As students are asked to reflect on their own work, they may develop more confidence in their own views rather than relying only on external authorities to reflect and respond to ideas they encounter. In addition, if students include discussions in their SSEs on the ways learning might continue after the class ends, they frequently recognize that they have learned more than is stated in the class syllabus:

> I don't know what my major will be, but what I have learned about critical thinking, working with other people in groups or as partners, and being able to visualize things as they are being related to me, will be of benefit to me throughout my life. Equally important is the realization that I have a right and a responsibility to question what I don't understand or agree with. I hope that I can instill this in my son. ["Ways of Knowing" student, Seattle Central Community College]

Often when arguing for relevance in the college curriculum and for work that matters to students, we are accused of overly personalizing education, making it so idiosyncratic as to be ungeneralizable. A less dichotomized way to think about academic work is to recognize that learning is enhanced in all aspects of a class when students are involved in shaping the content of their learning.

When we allow students to choose research topics or other activities that reflect their personal interests, they can explore ways to find convergence between the class material and issues that concern them. Faculty too can select material that reflects contemporary concerns, particularly those of students. Such material may help students connect their own interests to the content of the class and make that association a legitimate part of the class assignments.

Finding one's own ground creates meaningful relationships to the material. For example, in a class on Shakespeare, students can be interested but distant observers of his life and writing, or they can see themselves in an intimate relationship with his characters and ideas by making connections with their own lives. In a history class, students can read and understand historical material and find the historical conditions that have influenced their own lives. To be at home in history, especially to feel that we can learn something of importance, signals that we have located ourselves intimately in ideas. In finding a convergence between their lives and formal knowledge, students may understand that knowledge is not a given, singular truth but has been constructed from the ideas and lives of other human beings. This understanding invites students into the heart of the intellectual process.

We have also used nonwritten exercises to encourage student development of self-reflection and criticism. Discussions that engage students with the topics and with one another can help refine some of these skills. Whether these discussions happen in a large group during class time, in small student groups for a more focused discussion of class material, or outside class in an exploration of certain topics or questions, the important element is the active engagement of students in the discussion of their own ideas and responses to the assigned material. If we ask students not only to articulate their positions but also to reflect on how and why they have formed these opinions, we can nurture the development of self-reflection. These are simple suggestions; the members of a class could come up with many more that would probably be better suited to the interests and schedules of the class members themselves.

Students also learn a great deal about creating work that matters to them by reading the self-reflective writing of others. There is an abundance of such material today. When we expose students to the self-conscious revelations of authors, they become familiar with the practices embedded in scholarship that are typically hidden from them. In a program in political economy at The Evergreen State College, one of us wanted students to be exposed to authors who discussed—in historical, political, and cultural terms—relationships between their scholarship and their lives. The reading in the first week included Ann Ferguson's introduction to her book *Sexual Democracy,* along with three other such examples. Ferguson's writing illustrates these connections well:

> Because stages of my theoretical development mirror the historical changes in U.S. feminist theory in the 1970s and 1980s, this book may be seen as a personal odyssey through the major feminist disputes of the period. The theoretical is the personal in the sense that the creation of a social theory is a creation of a self-meaning for the author and her intended audience. Thus I decided to write this introduction on two levels: first giving a history of personal and political experiences as background to my theoretical development, and then outlining how the theoretical and political positions I take in these essays connect to a history of the major feminist disputes during the period. [1991, p. 3]

Ferguson's self-examination of the development of her scholarship models for students the self-reflective voice and the essential connection between scholarship and a "personal odyssey."

Peter Elbow, in his charming book about teaching and learning, *Embracing Contraries* (1986), models self-reflection through honest efforts to chronicle his own struggle to understand the difference between his experiences while learning and his beliefs about learning:

> Needless to say these essays about the perplexities of learning and teaching grow out of the perplexities of my own experience. . . . Learning and teaching seemed natural to so many of my colleagues. They always seemed to know what they were doing and why they were doing it that way. But it never felt natural to me and I never felt I understood what was happening— whether I tried to do it their way or not. Too much magic, mystery. I always felt nervous, even afraid. . . . I felt this perplexity whether I was engaged in the supposedly straightforward task of remembering learning (trying to get words and ideas to go into me), or engaged in the supposedly harder task of figuring out new thoughts and ideas (trying to get words and ideas to come out of me). . . . I had always assumed, as I think most people do, that as students we should be organized, coherent, and know what we're doing. . . . I had assumed that input always precedes output: that first we learn things, then we can have ideas; that accuracy should precede transformation. Not having examined these assumptions, I didn't have enough sense to notice that my experience had tended to be the other way round: that I could get things to *go in* better if I had first been invited to have them come out; and that I could be more accurate if I had first been invited to transform. [pp. xi–xiii]

Passages like Ferguson's and Elbow's can provide models for the personalization of one's work as well as for the self-reflective voice and can be found in most disciplines.

Reflection. The ability to write SSEs rests on serious and sustained self-reflection throughout a course. To understand what we have learned and its importance in our lives, we must do a kind of thinking different from that typically called for in college curricula. Reflection happens most naturally when the content of a class invites involvement, when students are encouraged to respond to the material by drawing, in a disciplined way, from their life experiences. For students, creative reflection and criticism depend on seeing themselves as central to their learning, a feat accomplished not by a teacher saying that something is "student-centered" but through the experience of being at the center.

Some critical elements support and sustain reflection in the classroom. The most direct and obvious method explicitly links assignments to the lives of students. If we structure inquiry around issues central to our own lives, learning becomes compelling and relevant. Reflection transforms curriculum into work that matters.

Many SSEs reveal insight about this personal connection with subject matter, insight gained through reflecting on learning. In the following example, a student reflects on how a change in her choice of language while studying privilege and oppression reflected an increasing intimacy with her subject:

I ceased to speak in distancing, lofty intellectual language and began to use my vernacular speech. I realized the vernacular has a power of its own. Initially when I spoke of wisdom, or any of my other topics, I used broad generalized terms, addressing it as an intellectual concept, removed from my experience, residing only in my mind. It was the first conceptualization, a search for trust hindered by my lack of confidence. I did not yet feel secure enough with my understanding to make it personal. As I gained confidence and familiarity with topics it became important for me to speak of them as parts of my life that did not require validation, they were no longer objects of study, but subjects.

My understanding of what is important in intellectual inquiry shifted from the purely analytical, impersonal and exclusive (Latin), to a more personal and community inclusive (vernacular) approach. I hope to continue to bring these two languages and ways of thinking closer together. My goals for this term were to find some concrete ways of actively addressing the issues of privilege and oppression in my life. Having grappled with the questions of how to organize, how to create change within myself and impact those around me in my community I leave with an understanding that I must place myself at the center of discussions about oppression. I also feel as though I have more ground to stand on, a growing sense of history and culture, to bring with me as I enter into anti-oppression work which feels more and more like the direction I want to pursue. [Student on individual contract, The Evergreen State College]

If we wish to promote reflection and criticism, we must make the classroom a place in which student-driven learning can happen. For example, we often allow class time for writing that focuses on the students' responses to their readings, discussions, and assignments. If self-reflection is built into the class on a regular basis, it eventually becomes a condition for learning, as necessary as reading and writing in building insight. When students and faculty regularly take stock of what learning they have done, where that learning is leading, and what it reflects about their lives, a transformation of the educational process occurs, one that makes room for critical and self-conscious scholars.

Focused writing assignments, such as those suggested in Chapter Two and the appendix, can help us examine both the content learned and the manner in which the student engaged with the material. Minor changes in the assignments promote the development of self-evaluation skills in addition to the recording of interactions with the content. For example, "self-diagnostic learning logs" are similar to the academic journals that instructors often recommend to students. As in the traditional journal, students record each class or assignment, summarizing the main points and listing areas that are unclear. For each assignment, they record both successful strategies used and errors made. In addition, at regular intervals the students review these journal entries to examine patterns in their own learning style. They then use this information to diagnose strengths and weaknesses as learners and to develop strategies to improve.

Community. Learning, like any work, can be more meaningful for students when it is done within a community. Much of the recent work examining student success and satisfaction in higher education confirms that learning is enhanced when students can work in small groups and when the class fosters the development of "learning communities" (Light, 1990; Astin, 1993). The word *community* has its roots in two Latin words: *communitas*, "the association of people on mutually equal and friendly terms," and *communis*, "belonging to all" (*Webster's New 20th Century Dictionary*). The word *community* thus evokes a picture of the classroom very different from what many of us experienced in our own university life or what we create for our students. Too often the classroom is competitive, with students working alone, disconnected from the other learners and often from the material itself.

Most of us thrive when we have an interested and attentive audience for our work. Although the faculty member may serve that role, other members of the class can also be good respondents and critics. In a community, student learning is no longer an isolated and individualized experience but instead is mediated by meaningful interactions, which may draw out what is personally compelling for each student. Other students are no longer seen as competitors but as colleagues and partners in learning. In collaborative learning situations, students can be one another's best critics and can hone their own skills of self-critique.

A number of strategies can be used both in and out of the classroom to develop this sense of shared responsibility for learning. Part of students' work can be directed to "peer response groups," composed of three to four students who meet regularly to listen to and read one another's ideas. Criteria used to guide responses can be chosen by each group or by the class as a whole; the focus of their critiques can be the class material, other related events, or more personal matters. The crucial conditions for these groups are that individuals interact for a sustained period, that they become familiar with one another's ideas, and that they dedicate sufficient time to provide thoughtful responses. If the groups meet regularly over time, students become familiar with one another's work and offer sustained feedback to one another. In our experience, using smaller groups (three or four) and providing some initial structure helps ensure the success of collaborative groups, although it is crucial to honor the possibilities of such groups by allowing them to develop as the members choose.

Faculty can also design activities and projects to be completed by small groups outside the classroom. Collaboration is at first challenging and difficult for most students. They have to find a topic of common interest to the members of the group, discuss their ideas in relation to the ideas of others, and contribute to a commonly conceived final product. Students often have no precedent for making such decisions, yet when they are successful, students learn a great deal about arriving at a common topic for inquiry.

As they get to know one another's ideas, discuss the personal importance of those ideas, and provide attentive and critical responses to one another's work, relationships change. Some students find assistance and serious response to their work. Such interactions foster reflection. By making their learning public, students can gauge what they are learning against the understanding of their peers. This kind of collaboration can lead naturally into self-reflection.

When students have a greater hand in shaping their own learning and are involved in substantive relationships with other students and faculty, self-evaluations become one more way to deepen and enrich the learning experience. Ideally, a faculty member will begin a class by discussing the centrality of self-evaluation and reflection and then build such experiences into the ongoing activities. Frequent and regular self-evaluative activities, through which students comment on their learning and on what they think about their experiences, give both students and faculty feedback they can use to adjust class content, assignments, and schedules. Such activities also help students learn how to be self-critical:

> Up until this program, I've been used to getting the answers from the teachers and things on the board. You know, take good notes, pay good attention to what's in front of you. And pretty much feel cut off—you know, the other students are just learning, they don't have the answers. But in this class, I've

heard some *brilliant* things from other students. I've come to most of my insights through other people. I've really had to look at the way I've been listening to people, and my prejudices in shutting other people's ideas down, and of thinking that I know where answers spring from. ["Revolution and Reaction" coordinated studies program student, North Seattle Community College, quoted in Gabelnick, MacGregor, Matthews, and Smith, 1990, pp. 69–70]

Effect of SSEs on Students and Faculty

We have pursued the use of SSEs in our teaching because they place students at the center of the learning process. A shift in who or what is at the center represents a shift in relationship between students and teachers, between student and student, between learners and content. Responses to content, rather than the content itself, become the "center" of learning. The use of SSEs challenges educational stereotypes of students as "received knowers" (Belenky, Clinchy, Goldberger, and Tarule, 1986) and the premise that learning is simply remembering and assimilating specific content. Incorporating SSEs into classes presumes that real and lasting learning may happen through student interactions with the class content, with other members of the class, with their own work, and with their own life. When we stress greater reflection and collaboration, interesting changes occur in how students and faculty interact. Students and faculty seem to engage in more substantive discussions that are informed by the collaborative experiences they have had.

Many educational theorists view the learning mode that leads to synthesis and self-evaluation as distinctly different from learning defined by the acquisition of objective, factual content. Kolb's learning cycle model (1981), mentioned in Chapter One, includes "reflective observation" as an essential part of a four-stage learning process. Kolb postulates that the ability to "observe and reflect on experiences from many perspectives" (p. 30) is a central skill for a well-developed and effective learner. Like these theorists, we have also found that the ability to reflect is a critical component in the development of abstract concepts and generalizations. Reflection helps move learners to greater complexity and sophistication in their understanding of any material presented.

These changing views about "learning" and the relationships between evaluation and learning are receiving more attention today in the academy. Faculty increasingly share some assumptions about learning, which guide the development of evaluation processes: Learning includes more than gathering facts and concepts in any one content area; accountability should include the voices of students; learning is more likely to occur when students have a sense of ownership, engagement, and agency and are encouraged to move beyond the stance of "received knower" to construct their own knowledge; learning involves making an action out of knowledge, using knowledge to think, judge,

decide, discover, interact, create; learning succeeds to the degree that it grad-
ually assists the learner to take control of his or her own learning process. Student self-evaluation embodies these assumptions. The writing of SSEs seems
to facilitate some of these shifts in understanding the nature of learning.

The Shift in Autonomy. Both faculty and students benefit from the inclusion of student self-evaluation as part of the evaluative process. For some students, this process can "turn on" the self-motivator rather than the external
producer. Students find themselves engaging with ideas not to please or sat-
isfy the teacher but for their own reasons:

> I knew upon arriving at Fairhaven that my old ways of learning were going
> to be challenged, which is exactly what I wanted. I have always been an
> expert at memorization and regurgitating information to satisfy an instruc-
> tor or requirement of the class (i.e. grades). I have also for many years been
> silent, afraid of my own voice, intimidated by others' knowledge and ease
> with which they spoke. . . . I have learned to ask questions of myself and
> others. . . . I feel as if I've been gently forced through the material to ask
> deeper questions, requiring deeper answers and to realize that the learning,
> my education, will continue as long as I'm open to new information or ways
> of looking at the work. For the first time in my life, I feel as if I'm being edu-
> cated. [Summary and Evaluation paper, Fairhaven College, Western Wash-
> ington University]

The confidence in learning that emerges after successive experiences in
writing SSEs is reflected in the following evaluation, written by a fourth-year
student:

> A main issue this quarter, and in the paper I wrote at the end of the quar-
> ter, was how I choose to view my experiences throughout my life and how,
> or even whether, those experiences are made into knowledge. Thus, my use
> of the terms "certainty" and "ambiguity." Certainty can come from the acqui-
> sition of knowledge as facts or from Knowledge, perhaps as in the case of
> Plato's forms. Either of these instances could give a sense of certainty in that
> the world is knowable and perhaps, predictable. Ambiguity, by way of con-
> trast, can see the world of facts and still view the world in a less concrete
> way. With ambiguity comes the mixture of ideas that may have previously
> been seen as opposing one another. For example, a mixture of good and evil
> rather than either good or evil. To be generally "aware" or to "keep one's
> eyes open" is to see the possibility of ambiguity. [Student on individual con-
> tract, The Evergreen State College]

For other students, the self-evaluation process can provide curricular coherence that links classes, transforming what was a serial and often discontinu-
ous experience into a new cognitive map. Through the self-evaluation process,

students describe not only what they have learned about the content but also new insights into themselves as learners:

> I kept thinking this would get easier once I wrote it down. It only got harder. I kept hitting wall after wall, coming to no conclusions with my ideas and my time was running out fast. A classmate called me two days before it was due and said, "I want to read your notes, let's go have dinner." We went out and ended up just talking about things we'd been afraid to say in class because we thought we were wrong. It dawned on me that these "wrong" things were the things we thought to be most important about the readings and they directly related to the questions on the exam. Suddenly, we both began writing furiously. We both had our answers. Before this dinner I had thought two things: 1) my writings aren't good enough to let anyone read, and 2) I do not need anyone else's input on my writings; that will only distract me. I was dead wrong. [Final paper, "Ways of Knowing" student, Seattle Central Community College]

The shift in autonomy affects the faculty as well. Inviting students to participate in the evaluation process requires a kind of relationship with students that many faculty currently find uncomfortable. If we ask students to share their reflections on their learning and its connection to their lives, in addition to summarizing the specific concepts or ideas developed in a course, then we need to find ways to listen to, honor, and sometimes challenge their perceptions. We as faculty also have something to learn.

The Shift in What We Learn. Reading SSEs often provides insight into cognitive and affective development, which may or may not have been an overt objective of the course. Access to a student's own description can give the teacher a better understanding of learning not easily tested:

> During this quarter I realized that to accomplish something extraordinary you've got to step out and attempt something you're not comfortable with. That one insight is worth any length of time. [Final paper, "Ways of Knowing" student, Seattle Central Community College]

> I do believe I have regressed to a certain degree this quarter. I could say that this quarter has helped change my goals, because it has, but now I'm stuck in that huge box called square one. The goals I started the quarter with have been dispersed in a new wave of possibilities. ["Ways of Knowing" student, Seattle Central Community College]

SSEs can tap students' perceptions of what is most significant to them. Many times, what students learn is not what we planned when we wrote a syllabus or planned assignments. Narrative self-evaluation allows us to tap the power of their language, their own "voices," to describe what happened for them in the class. For example, concerning a chemical dependency and domestic violence class, a student wrote,

> In terms of writers or others involved in the field, I was introduced to a host of professionals who are doing a great deal of research and work in the fields of domestic violence and voice. In looking at lesbian battering, I see myself continuing to read updates on what is being done to make services available to lesbians, and to follow the breakdown of the silence surrounding the issue in the lesbian community. ["Ways of Knowing" student, Seattle Central Community College]

Other students stepped beyond the syllabus and class requirements:

> Where once my world was black and white, good vs. evil, I am beginning to see beyond the need to draw boundaries in our thought processes. [Summary and Evaluation paper, Fairhaven College, Western Washington University]

> In a school like Seattle Central which has such a multicultural population, we are learning from everyone's cultural experiences as well. [Final paper, "Ways of Knowing" student, Seattle Central Community College]

> Within the learning of this rudimentary, building block level of algebra, nothing would be gained by my trying to assert my voice or inflict my opinion upon the proceedings of the class. I find that learning Algebra is like learning the most succinct language of all. If within this language I chose the incorrect "word," the "meaning of the sentence" would be totally erroneous. [Final paper, "Ways of Knowing" student, Seattle Central Community College]

Students can use SSEs to examine their own autonomous voice, their own ideas and knowledge, and their plans for learning after a class ends:

> Another important idea I expanded upon this quarter was my ability to speak out, to use my voice. This idea is probably the most connected idea of this quarter because of the fact that I've used it in every class and area of my life. In English, I was using my voice the second week of class when I read my paper on lesbian and gay youth aloud. In Japanese, I found my voice when I found the courage to talk with my teacher face to face about my grade at midterm. And at home, I found my voice when I told my lover that I needed time alone and I told myself that yes, I was a victim of all forms of childhood abuse. [Final paper, "Ways of Knowing" student, Seattle Central Community College]

Reading evaluations written by students can be an extraordinary experience for faculty. We have repeatedly found that students reveal more about their learning in SSEs than in their formal assignments. In SSEs students can discuss, on their own terms, the range of ideas and knowledge they have acquired, and they can candidly explore how these understandings relate to their own ideas and to their lives. Faculty members can use SSEs to understand students better and to modify teaching to support current interests or needs of students.

The Shift of Authority. Narrative self-evaluation gives students a voice with which they can not only describe their own experiences but also evaluate those experiences. In the self-evaluation process, assessment of the value of one's work is not just relegated to others. It is also required of one's self. When we decide to use SSEs as part of the evaluation process, we are not giving students control over the standards or criteria for performance. Rather, we are encouraging students to reflect on their own, to find their own connections between knowledge and life.

The accountability movement in higher education requires us to include the voices of students in the evaluation process:

> When I take a graded class, I can just live with the C+, but when I have to write a self-evaluation, I have to take responsibility for what it was I did or did not do that earned me that grade. It makes me confront myself more directly. The process makes me be more honest, both with the instructor and with myself. [Summary and Evaluation paper, Fairhaven College, Western Washington University]

Sharing the responsibility for evaluation with students gives them a degree of responsibility for their own education and encourages them to learn something about the nature of evaluation itself. As Wolf (1993) said when commenting on the connections between evaluation and learning she discovered in her research at Harvard University, "It is a moment when [the student] suddenly, painfully, or with delight, sees her work as someone else might, either because she can no longer dodge their commentary, or because she, herself, steps outside and becomes an onlooker" (p. 214).

When grades are not the only motivator for participating, students often find intrinsic reasons for tackling the material and concepts presented in the course. Additionally, they often begin to recognize their responsibility for experiences in the learning situation. They become their own critics:

> It is not grades that define me or my learning, a reality that I can easily forget at times. [Final paper, "Ways of Knowing" student, Seattle Central Community College]

> I learned that it was up to me to take responsibility for my learning and I stopped placing the blame on the course or the instructor. [Summary and Evaluation paper, Fairhaven College, Western Washington University]

The self-evaluation process helps make authority more visible and palpable to students and faculty alike. Even if letter grades are also assigned as part of the evaluation, no performance or achievement can be reduced to a letter; the student's substantive description also carries the weight of evaluation and makes the work real, not just a letter symbol. Perhaps this shift in the nature of the relationship between faculty and students is the most significant way in which self-reflection changes the conditions for learning and teaching. Where authority has traditionally been most manifest in the academy is where a significant change occurs. Faculty who urge students to be more self-reflective, to place themselves more centrally in their own education, must recognize and take seriously each of their students as individuals. Thus faculty must listen carefully to the ideas of their students, enter into serious and sustained conversations with them, and try hard to find ways to connect the assignments and discussions to the lives of their students. Rather than reviewing student work only for what it reveals about mastery of the class content, the faculty must also review it for what it reveals about the ideas of their students.

The Risks. Incorporating SSEs is not without risks and problems. We have seen autonomy and authority shift and have glimpsed some of the richness and texture of students' learning. There is, however, no guarantee that students will connect their learning to their lives and write honest SSEs or that they will feel "safe" if they do so. Because most students attend traditional institutions, which reserve to faculty final judgment about student effort, honest self-evaluation may seem dangerous indeed. Students often fear that they will be penalized for their honesty or, conversely, that they should write evaluations that reflect only what faculty "want to hear." The difficult task, for both faculty and students, is to recognize these dangers and then ask, "How do we proceed? Given the conditions of the institution, how do we do and represent our learning in an authentic and public way?"

Any attempt on the part of the faculty to make learning and self-evaluation "safe" obscures the very nature of their efforts—namely, helping students to claim their own work in the face of authority and tradition in the academic disciplines. Real learning requires courage. If we include only readings that do not provoke disagreement or ask only safe questions about what students are learning, then we may not get to the heart of the matter. Disequilibrium is part of the learning process, and self-evaluation often reflects this kind of struggle.

In addition to the tensions between the self-evaluative process and letter grading, problems may arise in faculty members' perception of the importance of student self-evaluation. When students take the time to write thoughtfully about their work, they expect and deserve a response. When students are involved in work that matters and when they draw in some significant way on their own experiences to inform their learning, they want to be heard. Many look to the faculty for informed, rigorous, constructive feedback. When they are struggling with ideas that may be confusing yet are centered in their lives, they look to the faculty as more than an evaluator; they look for an attentive critic. As one student wrote to a faculty member in her SSE,

> After two years of thinking about how people write, and trying all kinds of methods, what it comes back to, for me, is inspiration and other people. Not so much the image of another person . . . but speech with other people. Indirection and seeming digressions can be as important as purposeful direction—feminism has said as much for years, and yet it's still hard to believe the good news. I've really enjoyed our conversations this quarter, including some terrific digressions! [Student on individual contract, The Evergreen State College]

Whether faculty choose to write narrative responses to SSEs or to meet with students to discuss the evaluations, concentration and commitment are required. Some faculty provide vague or relatively superficial feedback or slip into the use of the clichés that find their way into all responses, robbing them of the personal focus. Other faculty find it difficult to be constructively critical. Their responses then become simply affirmations of all the student did well with little critical dialogue about areas that could have been improved. Both choices undercut the power and purpose of faculty response. Commenting on the degree of involvement by his faculty members, one student wrote the following:

> The faculty responses that have been helpful have been honest evaluations. "Well I noticed that you worked really hard here, but, here's an area or two I think you ought to look at." . . . I appreciate when the teacher has used specifics as an example of what they noticed about my work in general. . . . I'm disappointed when it's too general, when I look at the evaluation and it's only two inches. I wish there was more by the teacher. [Summary and Evaluation paper, Fairhaven College, Western Washington University]

Additionally, inviting students to connect their learning to their own lives and to examine the relationship of self to current and past learning situations can sometimes be emotionally laden. Many faculty are uncomfortable with the self-disclosures they encounter or are unprepared to help students confront the kinds of psychological issues that may arise. One faculty member confessed, "I was unprepared for the self-disclosure I got in so many of my students' papers. I had to decide how to reassure, refer, or confront in my office—not on their papers." Faculty and students may need to set mutually agreeable parameters early in a course to guide the self-evaluation process and devise appropriate resources for talking through the "unexpected learning."

Finally, not all learners enjoy or value the process of self-evaluation and the introspection it requires. Many do not take the task seriously at first. Some resist any movement toward self-reflection, preferring to relegate the evaluation to an external agent. As Taylor (1991) reported, "One woman described it [an SSE] as 'psychological ka-ka' and indicated that she would do it only because it was a requirement, but 'kicking and screaming all the way.' And, despite our suggestions for a shift in perception, her 'self-assessments' have really been program critiques" (p. 23). However, most students, when interviewed at the end of their undergraduate career, view writing SSEs as a valuable and important part of their learning in college. Through self-evaluation they develop the ability to generalize to other areas of their lives. They find that the ability to examine one's accomplishments in a particular environment sharpens the ability to evaluate oneself generally.

Changes in How We Teach
That Support Reflection and Self-Evaluation

If we teach by using our own real questions (those for which we really do not have answers yet) as a way to organize class material, then we place ourselves in the position of doing real work and of displaying for students how we respond to genuine questions. Working with students to address real questions will convey that they too have a hand in shaping the content of the class.

When the relationship between students and faculty becomes more substantive, students are more likely to seek us out for conversations and responses. To encourage a more elaborate and substantive exchange with students, we should be available, often quite spontaneously, for discussions about students' learning. By drawing seriously from our own lives, we can demonstrate for students how we locate our intellectual interests and then develop them. One of us, in a lecture to graduate students in her class, said,

Over the past year there are two quotes I have lingered over in my reading. The first is from a book called *The Passion* by Jeannette Winterson. She writes, "Somewhere between fear and sex passion is." She also writes, "Passion is not so much an emotion as a destiny." I have lingered over these two quotes approaching this topic today on transference/sexuality. *Passion* is one of many words—pleasure, work, desire, sexuality, love, eroticism (I will use these words interchangeably)—that swirl together. Out of that swirl comes my common, everyday notion of being "in love"; it is the being "in love" most of us learned about through our public knowledge of love. And like you, I have been in love in my life; I still am—deeply, passionately, sexually. But just as Freire reappropriated *love* to talk about the work of the teacher, so I would like to reappropriate some of the other language that speaks to the importance of work in our lives—that is, the language of eroticism, pleasure, and passion. The experiences I want to describe have no script to them. There is no telling where they may lead us.

Incorporating student self-evaluation challenges faculty to take a similar posture. If we ask our students for this kind of self-reflection, we must also practice it ourselves and take the same risks of reflective examination and critique.

As colleges and universities try to find appropriate responses to the recent accountability movement, many have begun to use teaching portfolios as a regular part of the tenure and promotion process. Faculty at many colleges and universities regularly write self-evaluations, addressing the formal criteria for required reviews or reappointment (such as teaching, meeting college commitments, maintaining intellectual vitality, and so on).

Other faculty also reflect on the significant work they have done during the year as part of a less formal structure, using self-evaluations to speak of policy and governance issues; they often go on to comment on conditions of the college. In the course of writing such evaluations, faculty members reflect on the experiences of the preceding year, often trying to think of the implications of these events for the college or for their own learning as a scholar and teacher. Just as the self-evaluation process often creates space for authentic dialogue between students and teachers, reflection on a year's work as part of self-evaluation process may create space for authentic dialogue between teachers and their colleagues.

The incorporation of self-evaluation into the curriculum fosters changes in relationships between students and students, students and faculty, and even faculty and faculty. As students develop the skills of reflection and a more personal and powerful relationship to their work, a different role for the learning community begins to evolve. Often peers become as important as audience and critics as the teacher is. Students look toward one another, as well as toward the faculty, for feedback and development of key concepts and support for their intellectual risk taking. These changes create shifts in both our choices about teaching and in the nature of authority in the learning process. Although the organizational dispensing of power does not change, the power associated with ideas and decisions about learning becomes more dispersed. This shift is inevitably quite uncomfortable at first, but it is crucial in transforming the most basic conditions in higher education. When we alter the traditional practices that shape the selection of topics and material, the evaluation of student learning, and the manifestation of that learning, then change is possible. It is change that allows self-reflection by students and change that honors the decisions coming from such reflection.

References

Astin, A. *What Matters in College: Four Critical Years Revisited.* San Francisco: Jossey-Bass, 1993.

Belenky, M. F., Clinchy, B. M., Goldberger, N. R., and Tarule, J. M. *Women's Ways of Knowing: The Development of Self, Voice, and Mind.* New York: Basic Books, 1986.

Elbow, P. *Embracing Contraries: Explorations in Learning and Teaching.* New York: Oxford University Press, 1986.

Ferguson, A. *Sexual Democracy: Women, Politics, and Power.* Boulder, Colo.: Westview Press, 1991.

Freire, P. *Pedagogy of the Oppressed.* New York: Continuum, 1984.

Gabelnick, F., MacGregor, J., Matthews, R., and Smith, B. L. *Learning Communities: Creating Connections Among Students, Faculty, and Disciplines.* New Directions in Teaching and Learning, no. 41. San Francisco: Jossey-Bass, 1990.

Hutchings, P. "Assessment and the Way We Work." Closing plenary address at the 5th AAHE Conference on Assessment, Washington, D.C., June 1990.

Kolb, D. "Learning Styles and Disciplinary Differences." In A. W. Chickering and Associates, *The Modern American College: Responding to the New Realities of Diverse Students and a Changing Society.* San Francisco: Jossey-Bass, 1981.

Light, R. *Explorations with Students and Faculty About Teaching, Learning, and Student Life.* Report of the Harvard Assessment Seminars, no. 1. Cambridge, Mass.: Graduate School of Education, Harvard University, 1990.

Taylor, K. "Self-Assessment: Discovery of Self and Self-Development in the Adult Learner." Developed from K. Taylor, "Transforming Learning: Experiences of Adult Development and Transformation of Re-entry Learners in an Adult Degree Program." Unpublished doctoral dissertation, The Union Graduate School, The Union Institute, 1991.

Wolf, D. P. "Assessment as an Episode of Learning." In R. Bennett and W. Ward (eds.), *Construction Versus Choice in Cognitive Measurement.* New York: Erlbaum, 1993.

MARIE EATON is dean of Fairhaven College and vice president for student affairs at Western Washington University, Bellingham, Washington.

RITA POUGIALES is a member of the faculty at The Evergreen State College, Olympia, Washington.

This chapter provides a conceptual rationale for the use of student self-evaluations in institutional outcomes assessment efforts and specific examples of some recent studies using SSEs.

Beyond "Mildly Interesting Facts": Student Self-Evaluations and Outcomes Assessment

William S. Moore, Steve Hunter

Prior to coming to college, my basic 12 year education from the public school system consisted primarily of math, English, history, and science courses. After completing 12 years of this sort of schooling, I could efficiently carry out the process of doing assigned work, although in a mechanical fashion without using much thought. There are only so many mathematical, scientific, and grammatical rules offered to students during high school, and the classes kept circling around these rules, or minor variations upon these rules. When I graduated, I knew it was time to widen my scope of learning. . . .

I am pleased about the changes within myself after only two quarters of the core program Society and the Computer. Because the readings took many perspectives on a given subject, it was necessary for me to formulate my OWN opinions. I no longer read a book and accept everything without comparing the author's views with my own or those already heard. I became critical about not only listening but following the speaker's line of reasoning. [Student Self-Evaluation, The Evergreen State College]

I believe that the changes in the ways one thinks about ideas, values, and problems are the main contribution of education to a person's life. Education should emphasize the development and refining of thinking skills, research skills, and communication skills. These are as important as content, especially in an age when our knowledge about the universe and ourselves is continually changing. There are also certain ideas and values that everyone

NEW DIRECTIONS FOR TEACHING AND LEARNING, no. 56, Winter 1993 © Jossey-Bass Publishers benefits from understanding, but too often the emphasis of education is on technical information and only mildly interesting facts. A good education must give students the opportunity to reflect on the really important issues of life. Fairhaven gave me this opportunity. I was pushed to go beyond the facts and think about their significance. I believe I now have skills and an understanding that will increase my ability to live a personally fulfilling and socially useful life. [Summary and Evaluation paper, Fairhaven College, Western Washington University]

The students quoted above are using required student self-evaluations to reflect on and synthesize their learning in college. These SSEs clearly represent opportunities for clarifying and enhancing student learning. Moreover, as Richard Haswell suggests in the next chapter, SSEs are potentially transformative developmental moments for students. In this chapter, we will argue that SSEs also offer a tremendous assessment potential for individual faculty, the specific program or department, and perhaps most critically the educational institution as a whole. SSEs, more fully than most other approaches short of interviews, offer a richer assessment window than more traditional and standardized approaches on a wide range of outcomes seen as essential to a college education but often difficult to assess—intellectual development, critical thinking, attitudes toward lifelong learning, and self-esteem, to note only a few. Our goal is to illustrate the assessment potential of SSEs through a variety of institutional examples, emphasizing the process used rather than the data or findings.

Evolution of Higher Education Outcomes Assessment

Ewell (1991) suggests that the current emphasis on outcomes assessment in higher education has its origins in the convergence of two distinct trends. One, from within the education community, focuses on educational improvement; the other, from outside the academy, focuses on public accountability. The improvement focus grew out of the work of such scholars and reformers as Astin (1985), Bowen (1977), and Ewell (1984) and may be expressed most clearly in two major reports on the state of American higher education. The National Institute of Education study panel report (1984), *Involvement in Learning*, had three major recommendations: Involve students in their learning, set high expectations, and assess and provide feedback. The American Association of Colleges report, *Integrity in the College Curriculum* (1985), referred to colleges' failure to assess adequately the impacts of their teaching as "scandalous." These reports reflected and underscored Astin's major argument that the traditional definition of educational quality as a simple function of an institution's resources (endowment, Ph.D.'s on the faculty, and so on) or public reputation was not particularly meaningful and that we needed to focus on an institution's contributions to students' lives and learning.

From an external perspective, policy makers and the public initially had focused on the reform of primary and secondary education. In the 1980s, legislators and policy makers became increasingly concerned about the rising costs of higher education and the complexity of monitoring institutions. As a result, assessment and educational reform initiatives shifted to higher education as well. Texas, Florida, and Tennessee were among the states to undertake an early statewide assessment effort; by 1991, all but ten states had some form of assessment initiative.

The early efforts borrowed heavily from the standardized testing approaches most common in K-12 assessment at the time. In recent years, however, influenced by leadership from the American Association for Higher Education and the relative success of decentralized mandates in states like Virginia and Washington, statewide assessment initiatives have tended to focus on faculty-driven, institution-centered questions about learning rather than state-defined goals and tests. As Hutchings and Marchese (1990) explain,

assessment is best understood as *a set of questions* . . . about student learning:

- What is the college's contribution to student learning?
- Do our graduates know and can they do what our degrees imply?
- What do the course and instruction we provide add up to for students? Are they learning what we are teaching?
- What knowledge and abilities do we intend that students acquire? Do they have opportunities to do so?
- How can the quantity and quality of student learning be improved? [p. 14]

Now outcomes assessment activities are as varied as the range of higher education institutions involved. They include, but are not limited to, interviews, portfolios of student work over time, follow-up student and alumni surveys, departmental capstone courses or exams, classroom research, transcript analyses, standardized tests, and locally designed instruments tailored to specific institutional or program learning goals.

Layers of Learning. Unfortunately, all too often the missing element in institutional assessment efforts, even with relatively enlightened institutions and educators, is the student. As Marton and Svensson (1979) have observed, the learning experience has three distinct layers:

- Content of the learning: an objective description of what was learned
- Context of the learning: relationships of various parts; how what is being learned fits into a larger framework, with one's own life and experiences, or with other topics or areas of concern
- Perceptions of the process of learning: the student's subjective reflections about the learning, the personal relationship to the discipline or body of knowledge, and metacognition about his or her learning process.

Marton and Svensson argue that to understand student learning fully we need to understand all three of these areas, not just from the "outside" but from the "inside" as well. That is, we need a description not just of how the learner or learning appears to the faculty member or researcher but of how the learning process appears to and is understood by the learner. In many instances, knowing whether students can recite the correct meaning of particular concepts is not as illuminating as clarifying the meanings that students actually have. Understanding these meanings can help faculty assess students' difficulties in arriving at the correct meaning—but a typical multiple-choice test does not address this perspective.

Taxonomy of Potential SSE Uses. SSEs can contribute to our understanding of all three dimensions of student learning on two distinct levels—the individual and the institution—and from two different perspectives—research and assessment. The four possible combinations suggested by this taxonomy are displayed in Table 5.1. The levels reflect two contrasting arenas: the student's personal learning, in a given class or overall, and the institution's influence on the learning outcomes of students. For our purposes, the distinction between research and assessment perspectives suggests a difference in the intended ends of the work involved. Research efforts pursue findings generalizable across higher education settings; assessment activities seek context-specific information useful for local planning and decision making and are therefore closer to traditional educational evaluation or action research.

Quadrant 1: individual focus, research perspective. From a research perspective, the focus on the individual provides a potential source of important information on developmental patterns in learning: Who learns what? when? how? why? Alverno College (in Milwaukee, Wisconsin) has for twenty years been a leader in the use of student self-assessments across all four of the quadrants defined by Table 5.1. Most recently, Alverno researchers (Mentkowski, Rogers,

Table 5.1. Role of SSEs in Understanding Student Learning Outcomes

Focus	Perspective	
	Research	*Assessment*
Individual	(1) Intra- and interpersonal change patterns of learning and development (who? what? when?)	(2) Student learning performance, feedback, and classroom assessment
Institutional	(3) Environmental influences on learning (how? why?)	(4) Broad learning goals for program evaluation and curricular improvement (outcomes and process)

Deemer, and Ben-Ur, 1992) have begun to study patterns of intrapersonal and interpersonal change through the college years and beyond, using a variety of assessment data sources, including SSEs. This particular kind of research does not serve individual students directly, but it does enrich and deepen our understanding of the processes of student learning as well as inform the evolution of the existing models of student development (for example, see Mentkowski, 1990, regarding the Perry scheme).

Quadrant 2: individual focus, assessment perspective. The individual level is important because of the learning opportunity inherent in the self-evaluation and self-reflection process described in earlier chapters. Formal SSEs work well in that context for assessment and feedback. Moreover, informal SSEs play a major part in the classroom assessment effort that was popularized by Cross and Angelo (1988). "Classroom research" includes a wide variety of simple yet powerful techniques. For instance, in the one-minute paper, students respond on a three-by-five card at the end of a particular class session to questions about what they learned that day and which issues or topics were still confusing or unclear. "The purpose of classroom research is to provide continuous feedback on what students know and learn, so that teachers and students can relate to one another by making all those little connections that move teaching and learning closer together. . . . It enables teachers to collect information relevant to their subject matter and their students and to *use* that information to improve the effectiveness of that teaching" (Cross, 1988, p. 4).

Quadrant 3: institutional focus, research perspective. Other research questions accessible through student self-evaluation relate to the institutional focus: What are the key environmental influences on student learning and development? for which students, under what circumstances? What do students perceive to be the most significant triggers for their own learning? Considerable indirect data exist about these influences (Pascarella and Terenzini, 1991). However, few studies have focused on the student's "inside" perspective. Once again, student self-evaluation could contribute in significant ways to understanding the interaction between person and environment in higher education (for instance, see Attinasi, 1990–91).

Quadrant 4: institutional focus, assessment perspective. The primary emphasis of this chapter is the fourth quadrant of Table 5.1: How can SSEs be used to make inferences about broad learning outcomes and perceptions of the overall learning environment as a way of providing feedback to the college or university? This work could take place in a broad general education context or in a narrow program or departmental context. One of the benefits of using student self-evaluation is its flexibility in addressing a wide variety of learning outcomes. The work cited in this chapter represents some of the best, and certainly most current, uses of student self-evaluation in institutional outcomes assessment.

Current Assessment Efforts Involving Student Self-Evaluations

Student self-evaluation is used in a wide variety of settings and institutional assessment contexts. At present, however, student self-evaluation seems to be used in three primary areas: broad learning outcomes, intellectual development, and writing or rhetorical effectiveness.

Assessing Broad Learning Outcomes. A major emphasis in higher education assessment efforts around the country has been the definition and assessment of broad learning goals, particularly of such significant and complex outcomes as critical thinking and interpersonal effectiveness. Student self-evaluation has great potential for demonstrating student progress on goals like these, which are often difficult to assess with "off-the-shelf" measures.

The "Ways of Knowing" course developed by Carl Waluconis at Seattle Central Community College, described in Chapter Two, allows students and faculty to use student self-evaluation to assess individual learning goals. Because these SSEs reflect on learning in classes throughout the curriculum, they also offer the institution an illuminating perspective on broad learning outcomes (Waluconis, 1990b).

For the "Ways of Knowing" course, students write a variety of SSEs about their learning in other courses being taken simultaneously. A group of faculty then read a sampling of the SSEs for the presence or absence of the institution's desired learning outcomes. Specifically, they evaluate whether the SSEs contain ideas about the fulfillment of goals and objectives, explore methods of learning, supply detailed examples to support ideas, show the student's relationship to the content of course, discuss a new perspective gained or old one supported, and discuss the relationship of learning to life, school, job, friends, family, and work (Eaton and Waluconis, 1991). The results of the pilot study indicated that this kind of material could be analyzed successfully for broad learning outcomes (Waluconis, 1990b).

Another Seattle Central Community College study moved beyond the "Ways of Knowing" class to examine SSEs written by students in the college's interdisciplinary learning community program (Waluconis, 1990a). The faculty involved in this study were interested in exploring the degree to which this program was enabling students to progress toward broad learning goals defined by the institution. The goals, derived and modified from an elaborate grid of learning outcomes previously developed for the college as part of an institutional focus on outcomes assessment, were the following (with examples from Seattle Central student SSEs drawn from Waluconis, 1990a):

• Gains in a sense of self and community, including self-esteem, teamwork, and community building

> This class has sure worked its way into the fabric of my life. Or actually it's
> just brought out things in me and other people which were already there,

but we never knew how to talk about them among ourselves until we had the class in common.

- Knowledge of ideas and experience, and associations and connections between and among them

    I have gained a better understanding of science and its workings. . . . I learned that science is not the malignant, self-supportive beast I had reckoned it to be. Science . . . is only as bad (or good) as the person uncovering its mysteries.

- Skills for becoming a lifelong learner, including an exploring, questioning attitude, knowledge of how to learn, and the ability to learn from mistakes

    I think I will be more prepared for my classes in the future because of this class. It has showed me that I need a lot more control and discipline to succeed, not only in school but in life.

- "Fundamentals," including reading, writing, and computational and keyboard skills

    It wasn't until this quarter that I received an "A" on a math test. You can't believe how that makes me feel. . . . My understanding of percentages and fractions has improved a great deal and also my problem solving skills.

In developing the rating criteria for these dimensions, the faculty also discovered striking comments by students that were not easily categorized but signified some kind of special learning. This fifth category was labeled "splendids":

    Now, fortified with the hoe of rational thinking in one hand, the spade of justice in the other, I am ready to conquer the various back lots of morality. I am anxious to begin sorting out the weeds from the flowers, undeterred to dig deeper when searching out the roots of a particularly thorny bush, and eager to plant and nurture the seeds of curiosity. Have I overstated myself? [Student at Seattle Central Community College, quoted in Waluconis, 1990a]

The study confirmed that SSEs can be reliably rated by faculty for evidence of learning goals and can provide quantitative data for institutional outcomes assessment. For example, 84 percent of the SSEs that were rated displayed gains in sense of self and community; 78 percent described gains in the skills for becoming a lifelong learner. This study also produced more than just numerical data about outcomes. For faculty, reading the SSEs stimulated "the kind of discussion and debate which makes the idea of evaluation exciting rather than stultifying" (Waluconis, 1990a, p. ii). As the institutional report on the project concludes, "The numbers generated by this report can of course be used and/or argued in many different ways. . . . The more important discussion is that involving the self-evaluations themselves. We can spell out and name what we think the learning means, certainly an important task in higher education if we wish to control what occurs. However, it is the meaning the students are making of the learning which will finally 'spell out' what the learning does, and using the process of students writing about their own learning will help us to understand that meaning" (Waluconis, 1990a, pp. 27–28).

Assessing Writing Skills. Given the nature of SSEs and the increasing attention being given to student writing and writing assessment approaches (such as portfolios), it is not surprising that institutions are exploring how well SSEs work as direct measures of student writing.

Reflective Writing. In a study using SSEs compiled over recent years, The Evergreen State College funded an additional analysis by readers at the Bay Area Office of Educational Testing Service (ETS),[1] using a holistic rating system developed for the California Assessment Program[2] to score the quality of SSEs as writing samples. Evergreen elected to explore this particular assessment strategy for several reasons: The rating protocol had a reasonable overlap with at least some of the college's expectations for SSEs; ETS staff were willing to experiment with a new type of writing sample (the rating protocols were developed for writing samples generated by specific prompts not employed in Evergreen's SSEs); it offered quick turnaround at a reasonable cost; it responded to an area of assessment required by a state mandate; and it was an expeditious first step in promoting serious faculty discussions of evaluating SSEs as writing samples.

ETS provided California Assessment Program (CAP) rhetorical effectiveness scoring guides in three categories: Observational Writing; Autobiographical Incident; and Reflective Essay. The Reflective Essay rubric was selected for this analysis. A sample of eighty students who had graduated between 1986 and 1988 and had produced SSEs in each of the four (or five) years they attended The Evergreen State College were included in the study. Using the CAP scoring criteria, ETS staff assessed the adequacy of the reflective thinking in these SSEs for the group as freshmen, sophomores, juniors, and seniors.

One major finding was a tendency for students who produced high-quality SSEs/reflective essays as freshmen to continue to do so as sophomores, juniors, and seniors. Conversely, students who did not produce high-quality documents as freshmen tended to continue producing poorer-quality documents throughout their stay at the college.

In terms of measurement strategies, this study suggests that SSEs can be usefully rated on a scale of "rhetorical effectiveness," used in this example as an assessment of communication skills, by external raters at reasonable cost.

Portfolios. The University of Washington has recently completed a Freshman/Sophomore Writing Study, designed to assess students' writing experiences as lower-division students and pilot the use of portfolios for writing assessment and faculty development (Beyer and Graham, 1992). In addition to collecting and reporting on the writing they did for all their classes, the students in the study wrote reflective essays at the end of their freshman and sophomore years, focusing on the quality of their writing skills and their development as writers.

This small-scale study (100 students) proved so successful in helping faculty understand students' writing experiences that it is being continued into the junior and senior years. The study findings led to a number of recommendations now under consideration by the university, including a call for increased use of SSEs in "departmental and general education evaluations of curricula" and the integration of SSEs into "regular course evaluation procedures" (Beyer and Graham, 1992, p. 4).

Composition Skills. The Evergreen State College has also employed SSEs for assessment of improvement in composition skills. Using suggestions by the director of Evergreen's writing center, ETS readers developed a holistic scoring protocol built on three rating criteria: organization of content, style/voice, and grammatical conventions. Holistic scores, from 1 ("poor") to 4 ("very good to excellent"), were provided for SSEs written in the freshman through senior years, by 165 graduates who had attended only Evergreen.

In contrast to the reflective writing analysis cited above, this analysis measured significant improvement between the freshman and senior years. Freshman-to-sophomore gain and junior-to-senior gain were found to be significantly related to overall gain. High school grade-point averages were positively related to composition ratings throughout the students' four years at Evergreen. Male freshmen tended to receive lower composition scores than older male students (Thompson, 1992).

This study provides an example of how SSEs can be used to assess student writing skill development. Perhaps most worthy of note for those considering similar analyses is the willingness of the Bay Area Essay Reading Office at ETS to collaborate in the development of an institution-specific scoring system. Understandably, ETS does not extend assurances about the reliability of such ad hoc measures. As stated earlier, the costs of ETS services are reasonable and vary according to the length of the document and stipulations for multiple readings and ratings.

Writing and Thinking. The same study of 165 graduates of The Evergreen State College assessed SSEs through a combined approach examining composition skills, communication skills, and cognitive complexity (Thompson, 1992). Three quantitative measures—holistic scores on composition and rhetorical effectiveness (cited above) and Perry scheme ratings (described below)— were analyzed separately. Substantial overlap was noted among the three measures. An index combining the three scores was constructed and analyzed, and the SSEs were qualitatively grouped as low, medium, and high on this index. The combination of quantitative analysis and qualitative interpretation produced a set of conclusions and recommendations about the interdependent development of writing and thinking skills as evidenced in SSEs.

This study may be of particular interest to those willing to experiment with combined quantitative and qualitative research methods and to those who suspect that the development of critical thinking and high-quality writing skills is inextricably bound. Perhaps the value of such an approach is stated best by the researcher: "If . . . the criteria seem reasonable or even consensual regarding writing and thinking skills included in liberal arts and sciences education, then [by employing these assessment strategies]: one can use existing measures and already trained raters; one can combine scales to reduce one-dimensionality and increase complexity; and one can then look at Evergreen student writing itself in order to generate 'thick description' and interpretation. The interpretation may point to deficiencies that can be improved upon and strengths that can be cultivated" (Thompson, 1992, p. 6).

Assessing Intellectual Development. The Perry scheme of intellectual and ethical development (1970, 1981) emerged from exhaustive qualitative analyses of the ways in which the students seemed to describe their experiences and transformations over their college years. Nine distinct "positions"— positions from which to view the world—were discerned in students' common paths through the college experience. Positions 1 through 5 describe the primarily intellectual portion of the scheme: systematic, cognitive-structural change toward increasing differentiation and complexity. In positions 6 through 9, the primary focus shifts to what Perry calls ethical concerns in the classical Greek sense: issues of identity and commitments, elaborations on a theme of personal meaning in a relativistic world.

Overall, the Perry scheme reflects two central, interwoven dynamics: confronting and coping with diversity and uncertainty; and the attendant evolution of meaning-making about learning, authority (the teacher), and self. Learners cycle through three increasingly complex encounters with diversity, and as they do, their meaning-making evolves. Most significantly, knowledge becomes increasingly conjectural and uncertain, open to (and requiring) interpretation. This central epistemology about knowledge and learning triggers parallel shifts in the learner's views about the role of the teacher, from authority as the source of "truth" to authority as a resource with specific expertise to share. The role of the student shifts as well, from a passive receptor of facts to an active agent in defining arguments and creating new "knowledge."

The meaning-making reflected in the Perry scheme plays a critical role in the learning process, and the model itself is philosophically compatible with the orientation to student self-evaluation expressed throughout this volume. In particular, the Perry framework interweaves the two significant aspects— critical thinking and synthesis on the one hand, "voice" and sense of self (personal agency) on the other—of the intellectual and personal development strands noted in Chapter One. SSEs seem to be an ideal way, short of expensive and time-consuming interviews, of tapping these Perry scheme perspectives, and several institutional projects have been recently completed or are in process assessing intellectual development through SSEs. In each case, the SSEs were scored by trained raters using a process developed for rating the Measure of Intellectual Development (MID),[3] based on the Perry scheme and involving student essays written to a specified prompt (Knefelkamp, 1974; Mentkowski, Moeser, and Strait, 1983; Moore, 1988, 1991).

Using Informal SSE Essay Prompts. Daytona Beach Community College used a specially designed MID essay prompt (quoted in full in the appendix) as part of a project to assess an interdisciplinary learning community for first-year students, called Quanta (Avens and Zelley, 1990). An excerpt from one student's essay follows:

> Probably the most significant thing I have learned about learning during the Quanta experience is that "learnedness" is a continuing process of ever-increasing enrichment and complexity. To me, it is not a goal or an endpoint. This definition about learning has become apparent to me from the interdisciplinary approach of Quanta which facilitates learning about literature, psychology and humanities. My learning style is that I do not concentrate or put effort into learning anything at all if I do not see the subject at hand as comprehendible. I want to understand as much as is humanly possible about something—once I become aware of its importance and relevance to us humans! I have never been able to memorize hard, cold facts; if that is all there is to a class, I just don't bother filling up my brain with storing disjointed, irrelevant data. [MID essay, Daytona Beach Community College]

The student essays were rated along the Perry scheme continuum, but the open-ended richness of the student writing allowed additional qualitative analyses of themes or issues relevant to broad program goals. For example, in the student response above, it may be difficult to judge the depth of her understanding of the concepts and authors she cites without follow-up probing and dialogue, but it seems clear that, at least with this student, the Quanta program has achieved an even more significant and difficult goal for the freshman year of college: in Nevitt Sanford's words, "to capture the student's imagination [and] win the student to the intellectual enterprise" (1962, p. 15).

Using Formal SSEs. Fairhaven College of Western Washington University, like The Evergreen State College, requires narrative SSEs for each class instead of letter grades. In addition, students are required to take a capstone seminar at the end of their overall college program in which they complete a formal Summary and Evaluation paper. All these SSEs become part of the student's permanent file and thus are retained by the college. Prompted by the Washington State outcomes assessment initiative and an earlier project at Evergreen (Thompson, 1991), Fairhaven College undertook a Perry scheme analysis of SSEs from a sample of approximately 200 students, using the same MID framework used in the Evergreen study. (For a more thorough discussion of the technical issues involved in applying the MID rating process to narrative SSEs, see Thompson, 1991.) Clusters of SSEs were drawn from the beginning, middle, and end of students' programs, along with a subsample of Summary and Evaluation papers.

Preliminary data analyses reflect significant development over time, similar to the results found in The Evergreen State College study (M. Eaton, personal communication, 1992). This pattern of substantial progress holds fairly constant over a wide variety of subgroups, including those based on gender, age, and status as "native" or transfer student. The other consistent finding is that the Summary and Evaluation papers display sharply higher ratings than the shorter SSEs drawn from courses at the end of students' programs. This contrast suggests that the reflection and synthesis required by the capstone course and final summative paper promotes developmental movement—or that the form of the Summary and Evaluation paper reveals more clearly the complexity that was already there:

> I am graduating from Fairhaven College this spring with a liberal arts degree. My concentration is titled "Concepts of Human Nature and Their Social Implications." I chose to do a concentration rather than a major for several reasons. First, I believe that the interdisciplinary nature of a concentration makes for a more integrated and complete education; that the knowledge of specialists does not provide the scope of understanding needed to solve many of today's most pressing environmental and social problems; that the artificial boundaries of academic disciplines are sometimes even responsible for our problems. Also, I discovered that the issues which most concern me are divided among different majors, and never given full and serious treatment by any of them. Most importantly, I did a concentration because it allowed me to concentrate on several meaningful personal concerns, to understand them in their broadest context, without having attention diverted by the specialized interests of a major. . . . I was exploring issues that not only have social significance but that also really matter to me. Consequently, what I have learned has more than just an abstract or vocational importance; it also has personal meaning. It has helped me understand my own life. [Summary and Evaluation paper, Fairhaven College]

These studies, along with the earlier work at The Evergreen State College, demonstrate that formal narrative SSEs can be rated successfully using the Perry scheme and the MID rating system. The results are encouraging, given that the Perry scheme embodies key educational goals independent of the disciplinary area of the student (particularly for institutions with an emphasis on interdisciplinary studies and collaborative learning). The MID rating system offers a well-established framework in which to study intellectual development along the Perry scheme, as well as a measure against which comparison with "user norms" are possible. Using SSEs, particularly as they are used at Evergreen, is a promising alternative to the traditional essays used with the MID.

The SSEs are generally richer, more extensive, and more reflective and are collected in a context generally ensuring that students take the task seriously.

Issues to Consider

Although the use of SSEs for assessment purposes seems extremely valuable and promising, significant empirical work in this area is just beginning. Quite a few issues still need to be explored. Three broad areas of concern are worth noting here: the validity of SSEs as assessment measures given the dual role of SSEs as "snapshots" of and "triggers" for learning and development; long-term perspectives on learning gained; and cross-cultural differences in feelings about "safety" in self-disclosure and about the role of education.

Validity of SSEs for assessment purposes. If SSEs are powerful agents of learning, as this book has both explicitly and implicitly argued, does that role undermine the clarity of the learning "snapshot" displayed in the data produced by such documents? Responses to this question depend largely on one's philosophical orientation toward the role of assessment. If the primary purpose of assessment is evaluative accountability of some kind, one is much more likely to be concerned with the precision and clarity of the data. On the other hand, if assessment activities are viewed as an integral part of the overall learning process, one should be willing to sacrifice some clarity in the data if learning is enhanced. The same distinction applies to a corollary question: How does one really know that the improvement over time displayed in SSEs—for example, in the longitudinal data at The Evergreen State College— is not largely a function of learning how to "do SSEs" rather than "genuine" learning? If SSEs function as this volume has suggested they do, this question seems irrelevant. The skills required for "doing SSEs" reflect to a great extent the kind of "real learning" that college hopes to produce.

Long-term perspectives on learning. The emphasis on fundamental developmental changes in learners' perceptions about themselves and their learning raises another important issue. Such developmental changes are subtle and slow moving; SSEs collected during or immediately following an educational experience are not likely to reflect the depth and range of the learning involved, even in the best of circumstances. Anecdotal evidence from videotaped interviews with students at Fairhaven College at the end of a specific learning community program and then again one year later supports this notion. In the later interviews, the students were much more positive about the experience and spoke more eloquently about the learning involved (Eaton, 1991). Follow-up SSEs seem critical for tapping students' full understanding of their college experiences.

Cross-cultural concerns. In our enthusiasm to engage students in the kind of reflective assessment and learning experience represented by student self-evaluation, we need to be cautious about the implications for the enormous variety of students involved in higher education. The student-centered approach generally gives voice to students who are not always or often heard—whom Knefelkamp (1989) has called "marginalized voices"—but we need to be careful not to interpret those voices only by preset categories. For example, beyond the obvious difficulty of self-expression and writing in a different language (English), students from different cultures differ considerably in their visions of appropriate roles for students and teachers. They also differ in their relative openness toward or reticence about self-disclosure—and in what is appropriate to disclose and what is not. The kinds of personal "truths" shared in SSEs thus could vary considerably. Evaluating SSEs on the basis of certain kinds of self-disclosure or perspectives may thus involve a strong element of cultural bias. Although the studies cited in this chapter have not revealed any indication of consistent bias, it is important to raise questions of whose voices are being excluded as SSEs are designed, administered, and assessed.

Next Steps: Other Areas to Explore

As noted earlier, colleges have only recently begun to explore using SSEs for formal assessments of student learning outcomes from an institutional perspective, and much remains unanswered even within that narrowly defined context. Nevertheless, student self-evaluation offers great potential for clarifying and refining a number of other areas related to student learning and the college experience, including the following:

Intra- and interindividual change patterns for learning and development. Who changes in what ways? when? Are there particular composite patterns of change, and what characteristics, if any, define the students following certain patterns?

Context-specific (for example, within disciplines) learning and development. Do students' perceptions of learning vary across discipline areas? Are patterns over time different across disciplines?

The significance of crucial transition periods (such as freshman and senior years). Do these periods consistently show marked levels of development (as at The Evergreen State College)? If so, why? What is occurring in the "plateau effect" during the sophomore and junior years?

Links between ways of knowing and ways of performing. How do the reflective and metacognitive skills assessed by SSEs connect to postcollege performance and work-related competencies? How can these skills be assessed in the workplace and linked back to the college curriculum?

As noted earlier, Alverno College is pioneering extensive work on the link between its ongoing institutional assessment efforts—using both SSEs and other assessment approaches—and research questions like these. More institutions need to begin thinking about the connections between assessment activities and questions of educational research that might cut across institutional barriers.

Conclusions: The Transformative Power of Student Self-Evaluation

Lee Knefelkamp has argued that "assessment is transformative. . . . It provides a means for self-correcting action and for the continual expansion of our thinking about the ideas and purpose of higher education" (1989, p. 4). We believe that student self-evaluation represents this kind of transformative assessment at its best. Like the Perry scheme described earlier, it represents two crucial views of assessment: as a dialogue, something done with, not to, students; and as a reflection of individual meaning-making, a way of constructing meaning that in turn profoundly influences behavior. Incorporating SSEs into an institution's array of assessment efforts thus suggests a deeper understanding of assessment than the way it is typically understood. More importantly, the use of student self-evaluation signifies a richer understanding of learning and the purposes of higher education. Recognition of the significance of student self-evaluation calls educators to "re-vision" learning as transformation and to reposition students and their relationship to the subject matter as the core of the educational enterprise.

Student self-evaluation, like the best of student learning outcomes assessment activities, is situated in a larger context of educational reform, emphasizing "improving" as much as if not more than "proving." In this broad context, the use of the findings and results from analyzing SSEs will vary as widely as the SSEs themselves and the situations in which they are collected. Still, as we have suggested throughout this chapter, student self-evaluation provides an opportunity for better understanding students' perceptions of their learning experiences and achievements. Furthermore, it has potential use across all levels of the institution:

Classroom. Immediate feedback to individual faculty regarding the relative success of specific activities, assignments, and classroom processes

Program/department. A better sense of student-perceived links between courses in a curricular sequence; consideration of the appropriate sequencing of skills or performance requirements rather than just content

Institution. Perceptions of the significance and coordination of general education courses; the quality and quantity of student writing throughout the curriculum, possibly leading to writing-intensive courses embedded in non-English disciplines

Beyond this focus on institutional improvement, student self-evaluation offers an expanded view of assessment, teaching/learning, and the curriculum as a whole. SSEs represent the quintessential "assessment as a learning episode" (Wolf, 1993) and are well suited to embedded assessment approaches that fit easily into existing course and curricular structures rather than being an intrusive, add-on activity for students. In particular, given the current and growing popularity of portfolios in institutional outcomes assessment efforts at a wide range of colleges and universities, the work at Seattle Central Community College, The Evergreen State College, and the University of Washington strongly suggests that SSEs can be a centerpiece of such portfolios.

The SSE format is also extremely flexible, allowing for a wide range of outcomes goals and dimensions; the open-ended nature of SSEs makes them particularly convenient for the broader, more fundamental developmental outcomes of college. Although this open-endedness makes SSEs more complex to assess, it encourages faculty discussion and debate about issues related to learning outcome goals and criteria. In that respect, the use of SSEs is worthwhile from a faculty development perspective as well.

Above all, we believe that colleges and universities need to expand their notions of institutional outcomes assessment to incorporate SSEs as a way of broadening conceptions of learning in college, exploring in more depth the nature of the learning and development that takes place, and fostering an increased empathy for and understanding of students among faculty engaged in the assessment process—which, as we are defining assessment, is really all faculty. Most importantly, student self-evaluation reflects the vision of assessment that Lee Knefelkamp articulated in a speech to the American Association for Higher Education Assessment Forum a few years ago: "Assessment is about revolution. If we really listen to students and take them seriously, then our teaching and learning methodologies will change, and then our administrative structures will have to change" (1989, pp. 2–3).

Notes

1. The Essay Reading Office of the Educational Testing Service can be contacted through Barbara Voltmer, Program Administrator, Bay Area Office, Box 23060, Oakland, CA 94623-2306 (phone 510-596-5500).
2. The rating system was written by California Assessment Program staff and teacher consultants for the statewide writing assessment, California Department of Education, Sacramento, 1989. This development work was directed by Fran Claggett, Educational Consultant, and Charles R. Cooper, Department of Literature, University of California, San Diego.
3. The Measure of Intellectual Development prompts address a number of topics, but the two most widely used alternatives focus on a student's best class and a student's ideal learning experience. Ordering information and rating costs are available from the Center for the Study of Intellectual Development (CSID), 1505 Farwell Court NW, Olympia, WA 98502 (phone 206-786-5094).

References

Association of American Colleges. *Integrity in the College Curriculum: A Report to the Academic Community.* Washington, D.C.: Association of American Colleges, 1985.

Astin, A. W. *Achieving Educational Excellence: A Critical Assessment of Priorities and Practices in Higher Education.* San Francisco: Jossey-Bass, 1985.

Attinasi, L. "Phenomenological Interviewing in the Conduct of Institutional Research: An Argument and an Illustration." *Association for Institutional Research Professional File,* no. 38, Fall–Winter 1990–91, 1–8.

Avens, C., and Zelley, R. "A Preliminary Report on the Intellectual Development of Students in the Quanta Learning Community." Unpublished report, Daytona Beach (Fla.) Community College, 1990.

Beyer, C., and Graham, J. "The Freshman/Sophomore Writing Study—1989–1991." Unpublished paper, Interdisciplinary Writing Program, University of Washington, 1992.

Bowen, H. R. Investment in Learning: The Individual and Social Value of Higher Education. San Francisco: Jossey-Bass, 1977.

Cross, K. P. "In Search of Zippers." AAHE Bulletin, 1988, 40 (10), 3–7.

Cross, K. P., and Angelo, T. A. Classroom Assessment Techniques: A Handbook for Faculty. Ann Arbor: National Center for Research to Improve Postsecondary Teaching and Learning, University of Michigan, 1988.

Eaton, M. "The Canon Debate Updated." Paper presented at the national conference of the Association for General and Liberal Studies, Seattle, Wash., October 1991.

Eaton, M., and Waluconis, C. "Student Self-Assessment: Thinking About the Way We 'Know.'" Paper presented at the 6th annual American Association for Higher Education Conference on Assessment in Higher Education, San Francisco, June 1991.

Ewell, P. T. The Self-Regarding Institution: Information for Excellence. Boulder, Colo.: National Center for Higher Education Management Systems, 1984.

Ewell, P. T. "To Capture the Ineffable: New Forms of Assessment in Higher Education." Review of Research in Higher Education, 1991, 17, 75–125.

Hutchings, P., and Marchese, T. W. "Watching Assessment: Questions, Stories, Prospects." Change, 1990, 22 (5), 12–38.

Knefelkamp, L. L. "Developmental Instruction: Fostering Intellectual and Personal Growth of College Students." Unpublished doctoral dissertation, University of Minnesota, 1974.

Knefelkamp, L. L. "Assessment as Transformation." In Three Presentations from the 4th National Conference on Assessment in Higher Education, June 1989, Atlanta. Washington, D.C.: American Association for Higher Education Assessment Forum, 1989.

Marton, F., and Svensson, D. "New Conceptions of Research on Student Learning." Higher Education, 1979, 8, 471–486.

Mentkowski, M. "Relationships Between the Perry Scheme of Intellectual and Ethical Development and Higher Education Assessment." Paper presented at Reflection and Anticipation: A Celebration of Two Decades of Work with the "Perry Scheme." Washington, D.C., December 1990.

Mentkowski, M., Moeser, M., and Strait, M. Using the Perry Scheme of Intellectual and Ethical Development as a College Outcomes Measure: A Process and Criteria for Performance. Milwaukee, Wis.: Alverno College Productions, 1983.

Mentkowski, M., Rogers, G., Deemer, D., and Ben-Ur, T. "Alumnae Abilities, Learning, and Development: What Are We Discovering from Post-College Outcomes Studies?" Paper presented at the 7th annual American Association for Higher Education Conference on Assessment in Higher Education, Miami Beach, Fla., June 1992.

Moore, W. S. The Measure of Intellectual Development: An Instrument Manual. Olympia, Wash.: Center for the Study of Intellectual Development, 1988.

Moore, W. S. "The Perry Scheme of Intellectual and Ethical Development: An Introduction to the Model and Two Major Assessment Approaches." Paper presented to the annual meeting of the American Educational Research Association, Chicago, April 1991.

National Institute of Education, Study Group on the Conditions of Excellence in American Higher Education. Involvement in Learning: Realizing the Potential of American Higher Education. Washington, D.C.: Government Printing Office, 1984.

Pascarella, E. T., and Terenzini, P. T. How College Affects Students. San Francisco: Jossey-Bass, 1991.

Perry, W. G. Forms of Intellectual and Ethical Development in the College Years: A Scheme. New York: HarperCollins, 1970.

Perry, W. G. "Intellectual and Ethical Development." In A. W. Chickering and Associates, The Modern American College: Responding to the New Realities of Diverse Students and a Changing Society. San Francisco: Jossey-Bass, 1981, pp. 76–116.

Sanford, N. "Implications of Personality Studies for Curriculum and Personnel Planning." In Personality Factors on the College Campus: Review of a Symposium. Austin, Tex.: Hogg Foundation for Mental Health, 1962.

Thompson, K. Learning at Evergreen: An Assessment of Cognitive Development. Monograph no. 1. Olympia, Wash.: Washington Center for Undergraduate Education, Evergreen State College, 1991.

Thompson, K. Learning at Evergreen (II): Writing and Thinking. Report of the Assessment Study Group. Olympia, Wash.: Office of Research and Planning, Evergreen State College, 1992.

Waluconis, C. "Coordinated Studies Evaluation: Self-Evaluation Project." Title III evaluation report, Seattle Central Community College, Seattle, Wash., 1990a.

Waluconis, C. "Student Self-Evaluation: Outcomes as Learning." Unpublished paper, Seattle Central Community College, Seattle, Wash., 1990b.

Wolf, D. P. "Assessment as an Episode of Learning." In R. Bennett and W. Ward (eds.), Construction Versus Choice in Cognitive Measurement. New York: Erlbaum, 1993.

WILLIAM S. MOORE is manager of outcomes assessment and research for the State Board for Community and Technical Colleges in Washington State, coordinator of the Center for the Study of Intellectual Development, and coordinator of the Perry Network.

STEVE HUNTER coordinates assessment, institutional research, and planning activities for The Evergreen State College.

This chapter speculates on the connections between student self-evaluation and personal development. It asks whether student self-evaluation, compared to other learning experiences, may not assist and even further cognitive, psychological, and social changes of the kind documented by life-span developmentalists among adults of college age.

Student Self-Evaluations and Developmental Change

Richard H. Haswell

Teachers—well, some teachers—like to believe that students continue to mature during college. For the moment, let us believe that students do and ask an obvious question: Do a student's self-evaluations change along with the student? But if that question is too patently circular, we can ask a tougher one: What aspects of growing maturity should we expect SSEs to express? And to leapfrog ahead to the farthest, most polemical edge of this chapter, let us ask a truly moot question: Can writing SSEs help the student mature?

Here is a test case, two SSEs from the same college student, spanning four years. In the spring of her freshman year, the student writes about the reading she has done for the two-quarter course "Foundations of Human Expression":

> This program has helped me gain insight into the new areas of art perception, creation, and religion from the books we were required to read. My reading and writing skills improved in the winter quarter. I had completed all but five of the required readings in the fall quarter due to poor time management: I completed all readings in the winter quarter. [Freshman student, The Evergreen State College]

In the spring of her senior year, she writes a comparable SSE, about the reading she has done for an American history paper on the antebellum politician John C. Calhoun. Is this senior SSE more mature than her freshman one?

> I had some difficulty focusing my topic, but finally I decided to look at how northern historians and southern historians treated the Calhoun legend and

see how they contrasted. In working on this paper, I found that a lot of reading historians' books is merely reading the historians' own opinion. It is hard
to determine what might be the truth about what happened in the past, and
nearly impossible to find any author who is absolutely objective. [Senior student, The Evergreen State College]

Setting side the issue of bias in the selection (with "sound bites" you can show
growth, or regression, with practically any two pieces of writing), many teachers will find the senior SSE more mature. A historian would find the willingness to deal with secondary sources a sign of intellectual growth. So would a
logician find the questioning of human objectivity. A writing teacher might
note that the sentences are more fluid and complex. A psychologist might see
a healthy advance in acceptance of self. (The insecurity of the freshman shows
up in the unintended humor of "I had completed all but five of the required
readings in the fall quarter due to poor time management," which she would
have avoided had she been willing to say "I failed to read five of the required
readings due to . . . .")

I, too, feel that the writer shows greater maturity in her senior SSE, but I
would like to add that she also shows more personal development. Although
people on the street may see little difference between "maturity" and "development," I will apply the second term in its technical sense, as used in the
disciplines of developmental psychology and sociology. That usage has advan-
tages. For instance, later I will show that, with a little understanding of current developmental thought, a more profound maturity can be found in the
senior SSE than most teachers will detect. I will also argue—although on less
firm ground, as I have implied—that these two SSEs may themselves have
helped further that development. I trust, then, that teachers will read a certain
hopeful elasticity into the and of the title of this chapter. What is the causal
relationship between SSEs and student development? I want my title to
embrace the possibility that SSEs belong to that elite kit of instructional tools
that not only allow students to express personal change (whether taken as
maturity, development, or even just learning) and to become aware of that
change (see Taylor and Marienau, 1993) but at the same time also help foster
personal change.

Unfortunately, authors who use the word *development* in their title take
on double duty. If their audience is primarily college teachers, then it becomes
triple duty. First, before any discussion of the main topic—SSEs, in this
case—a concept of development needs to be agreed on. Developmentalists
themselves have trouble doing that. Some believe development is an
autonomous, cross-cultural, physical burgeoning of cognition and impulse,
almost synonymous with aging. Others believe it is a constructed, culture-
specific acquisition of morals and sentiments, a kind of social training. Still
others believe it is just a way of talking profitably about human variability.
Developmentalists cannot agree on some of the most basic parameters of their

subject, such as how long development lasts in humans. Some think it is over with acne; some think it carries on through liver spots. They can hardly agree on what an instance of development is. Is it Piaget's conservation of substance at eight, moodiness at sixteen, college sophomore slump at nineteen, job enthusiasm at twenty-five, religious conversion at forty-five, memory loss at seventy-five?

Again, before any discussion of the main topic—SSEs still—teachers need to be assured not only that development is still happening with the students in their classroom but also that it is happening in ways friendly to the teaching of their subject. It is all too easy for teachers to imagine that development occupies, in a military sense, parts of a student's self just as pop culture does, beyond their control and often contradictory to their instructional aims. It is no accident that the one use of the word *developmental* that teachers do agree on (as in "developmental writers") refers to a part of the student population they typically imagine as recalcitrant to teaching.

The Developmental Episode

The question of the relevance of development to instruction has long stewed among developmentalists of all camps (for entry, try Vygotsky, 1978; Chickering, 1981; Langley and Simon, 1981; Case, 1985; Brown, 1982). From this primordial soup, several basic elements have emerged, which this chapter will adapt to form its own working idea of development. The reader may adopt it or not. Actually, the following notion of development arises pretty much from the safe center of the debate and turns out not only amenable to teaching but in a basic sense dependent on it. In brief, this chapter will take human development as a continuum of gradual shifts in affective and conceptual frames, urged on by both inner and outer promptings, continuing well through the college years, and following sequences recognized as common in the culture. This definition makes three assumptions important for college teachers: that the personal development of students is somewhat predictable, that it is affected by influences from outside the person (such as teacher intervention), and that it remains unfinished or open to change throughout the college years.

Obviously, by this definition most of what happens in people's lives (to use a distinction made by Gollin, 1981) will merely maintain their current developmental position. But there must be episodes that will help induce movement along the sequence, episodes we can call developmental in the above sense. Take one instance, not quite hypothetical. Much of what a particular twenty-year-old male student hears in a course on European history maintains the intellectual frame by which he conceives of history, as a chronology of political, economic, and military events unconnected with the lives of ordinary people. But then he is assigned an essay by historian Hugh Trevor-Roper showing that the cycles of witch persecution during the Renaissance paralleled the cycles of

economic good and hard times. The reading of the essay becomes developmental if it helps induce in the student a new and challenging frame of history,
one through which he sees the emotional and religious lives of individuals as
shaped in part by social events. *If it helps induce.* It may not induce such an
understanding, of course, and speaking from long personal experience as a
teacher, I would say with most twenty-year-olds it will not. But it can do so and,
in this case speaking also from personal experience, has done so. Therefore, I
will call his reading of the essay a developmental episode.

What traits make such episodes truly developmental? Forty years of inves-
tigation into adult development, inside and outside educational settings, suggest the following composite:

Embeddedness. Developmental episodes involve change not in just one
horizon of the person but in several different horizons—intellectual, emotional,
psychological, familial, social, cultural. One of Heinz Werner's lasting contributions to developmental thought (1978) was his insight that personal change
never takes place solely within one level of a person's life but rather is "embedded," or connected with other levels. (For a philosophical exploration, see
Riegel, 1972; for analysis of the impact on ideals of college education, see
Heath, 1968.)

Frame change. Jean Piaget early established the related and equally crucial
insight that the only kind of developmental changes worthy of the term are shifts
in schema, alterations in structure (or frame) of prior understanding that allow
a person to make sense of things, to "construe the world" (Perry, 1970, p. 23).
Developmental episodes, if induced by teachers, involve more than just an elaboration or filling in of frames the students already have, more than just a learning of new content. They involve such a restructuring of frames that students
have to reinterpret both new and old content, at deeply embedded levels.

Vacillation. Consequently, episodes of development show a tense vacillation, as new conceptual frames conflict with old frames. This conflict takes on
many guises—for instance, as an inability to make sense of new material
(Piaget's disequilibration), as a sense of unresolvable contradictions (Basseches,
1984), even as a regression in performance (Strauss, 1982).

Coercion. Vacillation is not an attractive internal state. People do not will-
ingly enter into it and, once there, remove themselves from it by backing out
as readily as going through. Developmental episodes, then, involve an element
of outer coercion, usually in the form of a trigger plus maintained pressure that
force the person to keep facing self-contradictions, keep questioning current
frames. As a whole new generation of developmentalists now argue, reviving
an old argument of Vygotsky's, herein lies the role of a teacher (Brown and
Reeves, 1987).

Self-reflection. The latest contribution of developmental thought is that
episodes also require some degree of metaconsciousness, some standing back
from and reflecting on the process itself. Unlike frame filling (acquisition of
content), frame changing seems to require certain forms of self-awareness,

perhaps as a "trigger" (Mezirow, 1990), perhaps as the cognitive looping or feedback needed to solve problems in novel ways (Keil, 1984), perhaps as the shock of recognition that follows when one's new construction of the world begins to have a material effect on oneself (Meacham, 1981), perhaps simply as a natural reaction to new concepts forced by mentoring (Bruner, 1986).

Life history. If developmental change includes self-reflection on that change, then it includes, to some extent, reflection on one's self as having changed. Awareness of self-development requires a sense of autobiography, some picturing of the self as at once constant and under change, some conception and reconstruction of a unified personal past and future (Freeman, 1984).

Known sequence. There are two characteristics of developmental episodes that the experiencer usually is not aware of. One is the way the episode fits, at least to a knowledgeable outsider, into a sequential pattern normative for the person's age, culture, gender, class, education, and so on. Indeed, placement within a recognizable sequence of changes is the sine qua non of any change that we can call developmental. That does not mean, of course, that a certain change must take place at a certain age with a certain individual or that sequences will be normative for all cultures (Feldman, 1980).

Integration. Nor, in fact, does it mean that changes need to take place at all. Given the "plasticity" of the human (Lerner, 1984), no developmental step is inevitable. No experience is a developmental episode until it is internalized. It is not truly acquired until it is integrated into the person's maturing self, until it proves itself a step connected with later steps, perhaps years later, in the person's ongoing development. At the time, neither the experiencer nor even a knowledgeable outsider can tell. Only time will tell.

This notion of developmental episode with its particular composite of eight ingredients lies at the center of this chapter. I should be very clear about the notion. Developmentalists have not made much of an effort to describe everyday episodes of development; they have been more taken with abstracting the underlying "mechanisms" that account for developmental change or proposing normative lifetime developmental sequences. They also have trouble resisting illustration of their theories with flashy, road-to-Damascus conversionary "passages." But although few people remember experiencing such explosive, Helen Keller hand-in-the-water leaps in development, everyone develops. As the years slip by, we all travel through new perspectives and understandings, and not all of us travel at the same pace or as far down the road. How does it happen? If not by epiphanies, then it happens by episodes. The fact of such ragged but universal changes implies the existence of workaday moments of induced reframing. Hardly noticed, easily forgotten, soon lost if not reinforced, they still are worthy of the epithet "developmental."

Actually, I am not concerned if such episodes are denied the label "developmental." They could be called acculturation, socialization, or wising up. They could be seen as a combination of experience and learning; certainly, something comparable has been named "experiential learning" by David A. Kolb (1984). They may be located in an overlap of learning and development, the psychological site Sidney Strauss calls neither long-term, multiple-year spontaneous development nor short-term, minute-by-minute school learning but "middle-level" reorganization of knowledge occurring over days, weeks, or months (1987, p. 133). But I am concerned that such episodes will be thought of as abnormal. They are not. Episodes of developmental inducement may happen less frequently and less regularly than episodes of developmental maintenance, but both are a normal part of all our lives.

SSEs as Developmental Episodes

Developmental episodes may seem abnormal because they are difficult to document. They are not memorable because they are so normal. Worse, they take time to prove themselves. Teachers usually watch students for only a few months and consequently do not have sure evidence for development even when they are looking for it. Where the documentation exists, however, all eight basic features of the developmental episode usually emerge readily.

Consider "Claire," described by Carol Gilligan in her book on adult moral development (1982, pp. 51–57, 158–159). Claire was one of twenty-five randomly selected college students interviewed by researchers during her senior year and then five years later. Here I want to argue that Claire's senior interview itself was a developmental episode in her life (although this point is not made explicitly by Gilligan). In a moment, I will suggest that SSEs may function quite like Claire's interview.

As a senior, looking ahead past graduation, Claire feels deeply "confused." The topic of the interview is her coursework, yet she connects everything with her current personal conflict (*embeddedness*). Essentially, that conflict involves her desire to stop striving to be the kind of independent and intellectual person whom people expect her to be and whom her degree in English suggests she will become and to start being a person more like the image she has of herself (*frame change*). Her conflict is between autonomy and responsibility, between caring for herself and caring for others. Sometimes she wants to act in the image her boyfriend has of her as a future scholar-wife, to act independently and separately, "trying to be myself alone"; sometimes she wants to act more as she imagines herself, connected, "trying to be with or relate to others" (*vacillation*). Although she resists "categorizing or classifying herself, in part because she is trying to fight free from this war of images, her interviewer presses her (*coercion*) for more self-description.

As she talks, Claire is soon viewing herself from such a distance that she says it "sounds like somebody else" (*self-reflection*). She remembers what strikes her as a "turning point" in her life. "It wasn't a great epiphany or anything like that. It just sticks out in my mind." As a sophomore she had spent a weekend unable to get out of bed, suspended between her disillusionment with the way a family member had acted and her inability to feel or see herself as worthy of action. Two years later, during the interview, she senses a connection between the incident and her present dilemma, "a direction underlying it all" (*life history*). She looks back on her sophomore self as emotionally isolated, "devoid of feeling," the farthest from that connection with other people toward which she is trying to move. Of course, developmentalist Gilligan sees the movement of Claire's life history better than Claire can. Claire is following a course of moral development especially common among postadolescent females (*known sequence*). They first depend on others for a self-image, then independently construct an autonomous image from their own sense of inner self, and then arrive at a position of relational caring, where a sense of self is interdependent with an understanding of what others are experiencing.

Evidently, Claire's senior interview became one developmental step in the direction her life took (*integration*). Five years later, at age twenty-seven, she is working at an abortion-counseling clinic and about to enter medical school (not studying to be an English professor). In the second interview she is able to look back on the first interview reflectively: "The two people involved in that conflict were myself and myself." Things, she says, have "fallen into place," and she has a much more secure image of herself as "maternal, with all its connotations." She is continuing to wrestle with the same conflict of caring for self and caring for others, yet she has resolved it from a stalemate into a rich interplay of commitments. She is much more sure that for her morality involves "the constant tension between being part of something larger and a sort of self-contained entity."

Claire's senior interview, I want to emphasize, is unusual as a developmental episode in only one way—that is, because Gilligan's longitudinal study of it allows the ingredients to be seen. Given these eight ingredients, I can now argue that, as experiences in the lives of students, self-evaluations somewhat parallel developmental episodes, at least more so than do most other experiences that teachers shape for their wards. The argument can be supported with four basic claims, which the rest of this chapter will expand on. First, as an exercise of intellect and affect, self-evaluation duplicates the developmental episode remarkably well. Asking students to write an SSE often coerces them into the central activity of the episode: embedded, autobiographical self-reflection on conflicting frame shifts. Second, in self-evaluation students often translate a learning experience into the language of developmental episodes. When asked to reflect on a course they are taking or have just taken, students seem to imagine or conceptualize the experience through the perspective of personal development. Third, the writing of SSEs seems to engage students in work that observers of the human life span have found especially fitting for development during and after the college years. Even if writing SSEs does not induce development, it certainly supports development. Writing SSEs is a highly mature, highly adult task. Fourth, maybe writing SSEs does induce development sometimes. The very activity of writing them certainly produces plentiful signs that expansion as well as expression of development is going on, just as Gilligan's interviewing looks like it furthered the development in Claire that it sought to uncover. (See Perry, 1970, p. 27, on the possibility that allowing college students to discuss their growth may "strengthen or hasten" it.) All told, the evidence for these four claims may not be conclusive. Little in the area of adult development is. But I hope the following presentation of the claims will persuade some teachers that their education goals may prove friendlier than they have thought to the ways SSEs and development support each other.

SSEs and Developmental Activity. Chapter One defines successful self-evaluation as a learning experience in which students reflect on and evaluate, make sense of, their own learning in their own voice. It follows that, when students write an SSE, they also engage in a number of the activities of developmental episodes. (See chapters One, Four, and Five for other connections with development.) Most obviously, the response of students will be both coerced and self-reflective. Students have no way out of an SSE but to think and take a stand about themselves. Initially they may resist self-analysis, but as with Claire, resistance usually breaks down with forced verbalization, in part because resistance usually stems from self-conflicts, which once breached become the best impetus in writing about the self. In a classic developmental profile, those students who show the most resistance in a set of SSEs are often the most vacillating (and produce the most gratifying evaluations).

Less obvious but equally important, writing an SSE is an act of life-history construction. Students are asked to make personal sense of coursework lying immediately in their past. John Dewey (1938) would say this task means bringing writers into an active relationship with the world. But it also means bringing them into an active relationship with their own lives. It is one thing to have enjoyed a course. But to say you have enjoyed it is consciously to add that experience to your life and hence consciously to think on what that experience has been added to, to think about your past. And beyond. To some degree, writing an SSE is an attempt at integration. Chapter One argues that dealing with a course in personal terms means taking ownership of part of it, but developmentalists would say that it means finding which parts one will keep and use for later development.

SSEs are also embedded. Converting an experience into personal terms, translating an academic experience from the academic voice of textbook and teacher into one's own voice, always integrates the objective and the subjective, the practical and the ethical. As a result, student self-evaluation sometimes activates frame changing. Switching voice means switching perspective, and a forced, new perspective serves as one of the quickest routes to conceptual reorganization. Certainly, the hallmark activity of the developmental episode, frame conflict, need not take place in writing an SSE. Students can "make sense" of their participation in a course with old and comfortable frames, and sometimes they do. But as I have just noted, the SSE assignment certainly encourages the discovery of inner conflict. When it denies the students sole use of the familiar academic conceptual terms and asks them also to find personal terms—when they cannot deal just with grades, tests, and assignments accomplished and must also deal with teachers, fellow students, other courses, personal interests, and career goals—then internal conflicts arise and old frames (say, understanding the material for a test) begin to grate against new ones (say, questioning the relevance for oneself).

SSEs and Developmental Language. That these ingredients implicitly add up to something that can be called developmental is more than just an outsider's interpretation. SSE writers themselves make that interpretation, explicitly, through the language they choose. I mean not just the dialect of self-reflection, which is everywhere ("I noticed that I am able to speak in crowds better," "How can I improve myself?," "For nearly nine months now I've been enrolled as a student"). Nor do I mean the translation of academic assignments into the argot of feelings, beliefs, family, social relationships, and cultural context—a language amply shown throughout this book. There is the crucial language of frame restructuring. Old frames meet the unassimilable ("the most startling event"), old frames prove inadequate ("I felt something was missing"), frame conflict creates unpleasant vacillation ("I had the most trouble with"), frame reorganization sets in unannounced ("it seemed to click"), and new frames take on the guise of solvers ("at first I was puzzled") or the guise of saviors ("at last I have found"). There are also deeper, structural signatures, implying that writers are interpreting their whole participation in a course of study developmentally. Frequently, new knowledge is qualified as true or profound in explicit opposition to deceptive or superficial, an opposition suggesting the feeling of insight that accompanies frame shifting: "I realized that interpreting literature was not nearly as simple as I first thought." Sometimes whole SSEs are constructed to narrate this opposition autobiographically. The writer's present understanding is accredited by contrasting it with past immaturity: "I now think of [Emerson's "Self-Reliance"] as one of my favorite pieces and I wonder why I hated it so much the first time I read it in high school." And—as an almost universal peroration of serious SSEs—this construction of life history extends into the future. Writers select elements of the course as of lasting value or declare that the course has changed or confirmed career plans or pledge that something learned will not be forgotten.

At the deepest level, hovering sometimes above and sometimes below the writer's level of awareness, the central developmental plot of frame conflict can usually be found. The conflict may remain a tense, unresolved vacillation, or it may reach a brief moment—usually where the writers are most aware—of tentative resolution. But it is a rare SSE that lacks such conflict. Given the opportunity or handed the requirement to reflect on their participation in a course, students habitually construct that engagement as a morality-play struggle between different views—one familiar but no longer sufficient, the other new and enticing but not yet fully accepted. It may be a struggle to move from an expectation that one should pursue a variety of academic interests toward an awareness that achievement in some interests will require abandonment of others; to move from an enthused assumption that a discipline will be simple and tidy to an acceptance that the discipline is complex ("cluttered"); to move from initial ownership of a career ("my profession") toward the awareness that one must participate in it with others ("get along"); or to move from the drive to achieve new academic success toward the understanding that entry into new subjects will mean making mistakes. Dozens of other inner conflicts besetting college-age students have been well documented in the literature of adult development.

SSEs as Support for Postsecondary Development. So far I have been thinking of SSEs as vehicles allowing students to express, and through expression to maintain, developmental changes that have taken place in their lives. It is also possible to think of writing SSEs as a purposeful activity in itself, with intentions and demands that may be judged more or less developed. It can be asked not whether SSEs show development already achieved but whether the task of writing an SSE is a developmentally advanced one. The answer is that the task stands well along the course that developmentalists have laid out for normative, healthy college-age activity.

This chapter cannot lay out the rich findings of life-span or adult-development studies systematically (for surveys, see Chickering, 1981; Bee, 1987; Haswell, 1991, pp. 299–307). But the point can be made with a sample of the findings. One of the hallmarks of the shift from late-adolescent to fully adult thinking is the recognition that formal or purely abstract conceptual frames are not adequate to deal with life, which needs a more complex, more contingent, more pragmatic understanding (Labouvie-Vief, 1984). Done well, student self-evaluation encourages this shift, extending and in a sense breaking down the formal abstractions of an academic course by bringing in the personal and the social. Another hallmark of college-age development is that students adventure cognitively out of the security of single conceptual systems into a messy, contextual, relativistic world where two or more systems overlap and vie (Arlin, 1984). Again, SSE assignments ask students to overlay the conceptual scheme of their course with other systems that may or may not jibe—a private history, perhaps, or a different course or an ethnic moral code. Another trend, at the level of affect, is that college students develop from a leery and unreflective posture in terms of their own emotions toward a more accepting and metaconscious posture (Bearison and Zimiles, 1986). SSEs, of course, encourage writers to treat personal affect seriously and openly. Or take the ability to construct autobiography, which lies so close to the task of writing good SSEs. Adolescents tend to view their own past as chapters in a history textbook. They can cite places and dates but have trouble seeing a direction or pattern. Older people make their own past more meaningful, think of it as forming an ongoing story that can be built on and improved (Cohler, 1982). In effect, they take more control of their own histories, which is exactly what SSE assignments ask students to do. Other adult developmental positions assumed by SSEs are cited below. The upshot is that, when students take up in good faith the charge to write an SSE, they take on a task developmentally as advanced as any they are likely to meet in college.

In some ways, the task is too advanced for college. This is a crucial point and perhaps one reason why, in fact, one does not often meet higher-order thinking tasks like student self-evaluation in higher education. The advanced life-span positions I have been describing—pragmatic, contextual, relativistic, affective, constructivist—offer a heady critique of the position usually assumed by postsecondary academic disciplines, which tend to be logical, system-bound, absolute, nonemotional, and foundational. Hence the radical difference in two educational uses of the word *development*. Academicians usually think of development as progression within a discipline, as when they speak loosely of "faculty development" or of a student "developing" in her knowledge of ecology. This usage imagines development as advance within one conceptual frame, the frame provided by the discipline itself. Obviously, the way most life-span investigators use *development* not only differs from but challenges this definition. Their idea of development entails progression outside of disciplines, because it encompasses frame shifting. Advance in expertise within a discipline is only part of personal development—and a relatively immature part at that. During healthy development spanning a lifetime, one eventually reflects critically on his or her expertise, viewing that expertise from the perspective of other domains and life interests.

To the extent, then, that SSEs use advanced-adult positions, they critique coursework; and to the extent that they reflect critically on educational experience (which is, after all, their purpose), they express developmental advance. Indeed, they often bring to the surface the conflict between these two kinds of development—disciplinary and life-span—that especially seems to afflict older students. One student writes that her SSE "is kind of split in half":

> One half is a list of all the books I've read for that class, all the topics we've covered, and projects or presentations I've done. The other half is all of the realizations I've made, all the achievements I've made and a re-examination of the goals I set in the beginning. Did they change? Did I accomplish them? [Fairhaven College, Western Washington University]

Note the reflective distancing of the phrase "that class." It is no surprise that this SSE was written by an older student. We see now one reason why returning students often produce the most successful SSEs. Developmentally, they are more inclined toward the critical, contextual, affective, metaconscious expression that SSEs demand. We also see one argument—although perhaps not a popular one—for making student self-evaluation part of the core requirements for an undergraduate degree. A wise institution provides its inmates with institutionalized ways to develop free of itself.

SSEs as Inducers of Development. We have reached our most moot question. Is an SSE assignment merely an opportunity to express and maintain such developmental wonts in students (albeit an opportunity not much offered within academia), or does it also help induce development? There are two positive answers to this question. One is that the expression, the verbalization, of a developmental conflict always furthers development to some degree. Claire, Carol Gilligan's subject struggling to justify an image of herself that does not match the image others have of her, insists throughout her senior interview that she cannot "verbalize the justification." Yet the fact that she does verbalize it may have made the interview the developmental episode that her later history shows it to have been (Gilligan, 1982, p. 59). A stronger form of this answer—promoted by Vygotsky (1978), Lacan (1981), and Bruner (1986)—is that, as soon as humans have learned a language, no further development takes place without verbalization.

The other answer is more circumstantial, less theoretical, and less controversial. It takes its evidence from the students themselves. A day after writing an SSE for a literature course, for instance, students at Washington State University remember the act as if it were a developmental episode. They describe it as "digging deep," seeing the course "as a whole," dealing with "mixed emotions," "mentioning things that I *really* want to incorporate into my thought and thinking." They often remember the task as testing new and dangerous waters. It was "difficult," "painful," "scary." The sense of standing back from themselves to get a better view of their selves emerges more starkly in their memory of writing the SSEs than in the SSEs themselves:

> Kind of like going to the doctor and getting probed & not really enjoying it but you know it's the best thing. Only this time I was the one w/ the Q-tip probing myself instead of a doctor w/ coffee breath. [Washington State University]

Indeed, perhaps the most telling evidence is another disparity between their SSEs and their memory of writing them, and that is their frequent complaint that their SSEs did not really say what they wanted. They remember their inability to find the right words (always a good sign of developmental movement). The result to them now sounds "cheesy," "hollow," "forced," and, as if it were still a voice from a past they want to disown, "quaint." The suggestion is that the act of writing an SSE stimulates a kind of delayed-reaction advance in maturity, which—ironically but understandably—sees that fostering act as immature. (It is perfectly human to be critical of the mistake that fosters the understanding that allows the critique.)

A knowledgeable outsider, of course, sees a different picture and has little trouble finding traces within many SSEs of developmental activity taking place during and by virtue of the writing. Writers begin objectively, end subjectively. They contradict themselves and then notice the contradiction: "I guess what I am saying is . . ." They bring the course into the act of writing: "Reading literature from the 18th century on has made me appreciate that people who knew nothing of the computer I am typing on experienced similar emotions." They write in the open-ended epistemic mode of words leading the way to understanding:

> Did I learn from this class? Did it change me? Yes, and no respectively. What exactly did I learn. Well, for me the biggest . . . [Washington State University]

Most telling, they write pledges, often toward the end of the piece. In SSEs, the pledge serves as a verbal act of self-resolve to change or to maintain change: "This course is just an introduction to a lifetime interest, as I see it, and I will read more of . . ." In a developmental sense, the pledge is the complementary function of words as self-discovery; it is words as self-projection. Indeed, the ability to construct images of oneself in the future, to imagine "possible selves," itself matures with adults. The presence of pledges within SSEs may be another sign that the task is developmentally advanced (Cross and Markus, 1991).

Do SSE pledges hold up? To know would take longitudinal studies such as Gilligan's, studies of the sort just under way (see Chapters Four and Five; Taylor, 1991; Thompson, 1992). In the meantime, a tentative answer in the affirmative is provided by a preliminary look at fifty pairs of SSEs from The Evergreen State College. The first of each pair was written during the freshman year and the second by the same student during the senior year. Often, the conflicts shown in the first-year SSE are resolved or better understood in the fourth-year SSE. Consider one freshman's self-evaluation for the course "Thinking Straight." It expresses a blatant contradiction. Although the writer ends pledging to achieve his "eventual goal in the social sciences," only once in his 500-word evaluation does he refer to another human being. Significantly, the reference is a complaint that the insights of other students were so similar to his own that they "led to stagnated discussions and unproductive seminars," a sign that he must have been aware of his difficulty in relating to others. He wishes for better "seminar skills," to become a "more active participant." Apparently he helped make that wish come true during the next three years. His senior SSE for a criminology course devotes a full single-spaced page to discussing whether inmates in a state prison are "having their needs met." The direction from the freshman to the senior SSE, of course, follows a familiar life-span developmental route during the college years, from aloofness to greater empathy with others (Benack, 1984).

Another freshman shows a good deal of ambivalence toward a course for which he is required to read Aristotle, Shakespeare, Hobbes, Locke, and other difficult writers. Although he says they held little interest for him, he feels "that my exposure to them was beneficial." "My exposure" is a telling phrase. Clearly he is afraid he will not be able to cope with such challenging and famous thinkers. He singles out the academic work of comparing and judging their arguments as especially useful to him, not because of what he learned but because such methodology reduces his fear: "Now I do not find them quite as threatening." As a senior, this sense of vulnerability in the face of resistant intellectual material has dissipated. He "makes peace" with a difficult psychology course because he now feels that it is good to work with frustration and challenge. "Dysfunctional," he says, is a metaphor that not only describes the course but proves "very useful in understanding and conveying real life messages." "Where the real learning takes place" is not with achieved goals but with "frustration-producing structures," with the "process of working to achieve our goals." His freshman and senior SSEs show advance along an adult-developmental route especially well documented by Linda L. Viney (1987): from a need to find tasks that are readily solved to an awareness that self-doubts and half-completed tasks are an unavoidable and beneficial burden of the human endeavor.

Another student recognizes in her freshman year that a "personal issue" she has to "face" is "perfectionism." In the course she is evaluating, her teacher has given no specific assignments and no grades, and for the first time she herself has been forced to decide the limits of her course goals and the measure of her own academic success. Because she has been denied competition with other students, she is unable to know if she has "succeeded" and lacks her accustomed feelings of "satisfaction" with academic performance and "mastery and completeness within myself." Although the "challenge" of a self-paced computer program in calculus appealed to her, the freshman SSE converts her success with the method into self-doubt, and she ends up "disturbed" at her "lack of progress" in math, which had been a strong point in high school. Her need academically to judge herself by competition with others finds a hint of solution, however, in her discussion of freshman seminars, where she has been forced to let others pursue topics at their own pace: "It seemed at times we did not accomplish enough in seminar but by experiencing this frustration I learned patience." Four years later, as a senior, she shows what she had pledged as a freshman—patience with herself and others. She much more sets standards of success from within instead of from without. She no longer worries about her loss of math competitiveness and is happy with a review of precalculus because "my understanding of the concepts went beyond memorization of the theorems to a clear understanding of their basis." She sees as a "natural use of my talents and interests" her abilities to facilitate a dream-interpretation group, interview for a hiring committee, and listen to terminating psychiatric clients review their year's therapy. All in all, her freshman and senior SSEs show her progressing along that life-span path from other-dependency to self-actualization described so well by Abraham Maslow (1970) and Arthur Chickering (1969).

Or turn back to the freshman's SSE with which this chapter began (the entire SSE is reproduced in the appendix). Life-span developmental studies allow us to see an astonishing fact: In discussing the course "Foundations of

Human Expression," not once does the student allude to the existence of authors. Her freshman conceptual frame about reading assumes that books are so given, so authoritative, that she does not even think of them as having authors. No wonder that she identifies her main concern as a "fear of speaking my mind in a group situation." She must imagine that her words should have the same disembodied authority as the books she has been assigned to read. As a senior, however, she has learned not only that books have authors but that authors are fallible people like her. She can end her senior SSE pledging that her progress in "how to see more than one side of an issue, and how to listen to others" will be among those "things I can take with me and help me in the future." Life-span studies show that the maturity of her senior SSE is of quite normal growth for college students, who tend away from an unquestioned acceptance of authority and conformity to the beliefs of others toward questioning of authority and construction of their own beliefs (Kramer, 1983).

Integration?

Of course, the argument that student self-evaluation may help foster an individual's development has a counterargument: This particular developmental change, and the others illustrated by the freshman/senior SSE sets, are common to college culture. If so, it is presumptuous to think that one pedagogical method would have much to do with such changes. Christina Haas (1992), for instance, found precisely the same change in concept of authorship with a student who never wrote one SSE in four undergraduate years but who developed her more mature notion while writing a routine term paper in her senior year.

There remains, however, the question of how this senior will integrate her notion—how she will retain, use, and continue to develop her notion. Will she manage to "take it with her" without periodic acts of self-reflection, self-resolve, and self-construction, such as those SSEs demand? Over and over, postgraduation studies find college alumni unable to remember the great bulk of their educational experience. The isolated incidents they do remember, in fact, have the general shape of developmental episodes: embedded, frame conflicted, coerced, and self-reflective. Many are peripheral to instruction: being chastised by a work-study supervisor, facing up to a family crisis, learning to live with an assigned roommate. Of instructional experience, they may remember a one-on-one conference with a teacher but not any lectures, a forced rewriting of one paper but not any other papers, their own presentation before the class but not the presentation of a visiting expert, a field trip into a prison but not any essays read about penology. The basic ("developmental"?) lesson that student self-evaluation teaches to teachers is that no one can make a particular experience, including writing an SSE, a developmental episode for another person. Only the person can make it such.

But there is the point. It is easy to shape an experience for another person in such a way that the person is unlikely to make it developmental. Chapter

Five argues that SSEs work as an ideal method of assessment in that they both measure and allow learning. The developmental perspective of this chapter suggests that teachers will find student self-evaluation a model, a clear shape, for other educational ways to fulfill their duties as mentors and coercers—ways to convert the experience they want for their students' education into experience that will not be lost but end up part of their students' lives.

In the end it is best to be honest and admit that student self-evaluation is implicated with, folded into, personal development in ways that are not simple. The distinction between maintenance and inducement finally breaks down, as it should. True SSEs may ignore, bypass, cradle, safeguard, nudge, nettle, ignite, keep running, restore, repair, bolster, and generate development—or they may not. But they cannot stall, misdirect, petrify, or kill it. That is not a claim all educational practices can make.

References

Arlin, P. K. "Adolescent and Adult Thought: A Structural Interpretation." In M. L. Commons and others (eds.), *Beyond Formal Operations: Late Adolescent and Adult Cognitive Development.* New York: Praeger, 1984.

Basseches, M. A. *Dialectical Thinking and Adult Development.* Norwood, N.J.: Ablex, 1984.

Bearison, D. J., and Zimiles, H. "Developmental Perspectives on Thought and Emotion: An Introduction." In D. J. Bearison and H. Zimiles (eds.), *Thought and Emotion: Developmental Perspectives.* New York: Erlbaum, 1986.

Bee, H. L. *The Journey of Adulthood.* New York: Macmillan, 1987.

Benack, S. "Postformal Epistemologies and the Growth of Empathy." In M. L. Commons and others (eds.), *Beyond Formal Operations: Late Adolescent and Adult Cognitive Development.* New York: Praeger, 1984.

Brown, A. L. "Learning and Development: The Problem of Compatibility, Access, and Induction." *Human Development,* 1982, *25,* 89–115.

Brown, A. L., and Reeves, R. A. "Bandwidths of Competence: The Role of Supportive Contexts in Learning and Development." In L. S. Liben (ed.), *Development and Learning: Conflict or Congruence?* New York: Erlbaum, 1987.

Bruner, J. *Actual Minds, Possible Worlds.* Cambridge, Mass.: Harvard University Press, 1986.

Case, R. *Intellectual Development: Birth to Adulthood.* San Diego, Calif.: Academic Press, 1985.

Chickering, A. W. *Education and Identity.* San Francisco: Jossey-Bass, 1969.

Chickering, A. W. "Introduction." In A. W. Chickering and Associates, *The Modern American College: Responding to the New Realities of Diverse Students and a Changing Society.* San Francisco: Jossey-Bass, 1981.

Cohler, B. J. "Personal Narrative and Life Course." In P. B. Baltes and O. G. Brim (eds.), *Life-Span Development and Behavior.* Vol. 4. San Diego, Calif.: Academic Press, 1982.

Cross, S., and Markus, H. "Possible Selves Across the Life Span." *Human Development,* 1991, *34,* 230–255.

Dewey, J. *Experience and Education.* Toronto, Ontario: Collier-Macmillan Canada, 1938.

Feldman, D. *Beyond Universals in Cognitive Development.* Norwood, N.J.: Ablex, 1980.

Freeman, M. "History, Narrative, and Life-Span Developmental Knowledge." *Human Development,* 1984, *27,* 1–19.

Gilligan, C. *In a Different Voice: Psychological Theory and Women's Development.* Cambridge, Mass.: Harvard University Press, 1982.

Gollin, E. S. "Development and Plasticity." In E. S. Gollin (ed.), *Developmental Plasticity: Behavioral and Biological Aspects of Variations in Development.* San Diego, Calif.: Academic Press, 1981.

Haas, C. "Expanding Notions of Author and Text: A Longitudinal Study of College Reading Practices." Unpublished manuscript, 1992.

Haswell, R. H. *Gaining Ground in College Writing: Tales of Development and Interpretation.* Dallas, Tex.: Southern Methodist University Press, 1991.

Heath, D. H. *Growing Up in College: Liberal Education and Maturity.* San Francisco: Jossey-Bass, 1968.

Keil, F. C. "Mechanisms of Cognitive Development and the Structure of Knowledge." In R. J. Sternberg (ed.), *Mechanisms of Cognitive Development.* New York: W. H. Freeman, 1984.

Kolb, D. A. *Experiential Learning: Experience as the Source of Learning and Development.* Englewood Cliffs, N.J.: Prentice Hall, 1984.

Kramer, D. "Post-Formal Operations? A Need for Further Conceptualization." *Human Development,* 1983, *26,* 91–105.

Labouvie-Vief, G. "Culture, Language, and Mature Rationality." In K. A. McCluskey and H. W. Reese (eds.), *Life-Span Developmental Psychology: Historical and Generational Effects.* San Diego, Calif.: Academic Press, 1984.

Lacan, J. *Speech and Language in Psychoanalysis.* (A. Wilden, trans.). Baltimore, Md.: Johns Hopkins University Press, 1981.

Langley, P., and Simon, H. A. "The Central Role of Learning in Cognition." In J. R. Anderson (ed.), *Cognitive Skills and Their Acquisition.* New York: Erlbaum, 1981.

Lerner, R. M. *On the Nature of Human Plasticity.* Cambridge, England: Cambridge University Press, 1984.

Maslow, A. H. *Motivation and Personality.* (2nd ed.) New York: HarperCollins, 1970.

Meacham, J. H. "Political Values, Conceptual Models, and Research." In R. M. Lerner and N. A. Busch-Rossnagel (eds.), *Individuals as Producers of Their Development: A Life-Span Perspective.* San Diego, Calif.: Academic Press, 1981.

Mezirow, J. "How Critical Reflection Triggers Transformative Learning." In J. Mezirow and Associates, *Fostering Critical Reflection in Adulthood: A Guide to Transformative and Emancipatory Learning.* San Francisco: Jossey-Bass, 1990.

Perry, W. G. *Forms of Intellectual and Ethical Development in the College Years: A Scheme.* Troy, Mo.: Holt, Rinehart & Winston, 1970.

Riegel, K. F. "Time and Change in the Development of the Individual and Society." In H. W. Reese (ed.), *Advances in Child Development and Behavior.* Vol. 7. San Diego, Calif.: Academic Press, 1972.

Strauss, S. "Introduction." In S. Strauss and Ruth Stavy (eds.), *U-Shaped Behavioral Growth.* San Diego, Calif.: Academic Press, 1982.

Strauss, S. "Educational-Developmental Psychology and School Learning." In L. S. Liben (ed.), *Development and Learning: Conflict or Congruence?* New York: Erlbaum, 1987.

Taylor, K. "Self-Assessment, Discovery of Self, and Self-Development in the Adult Learner." Developed from K. Taylor, "Transforming Learning: Experiences of Adult Development and Transformation of Re-entry Learners in an Adult Degree Program." Unpublished doctoral dissertation, The Union Graduate School, The Union Institute, 1991.

Taylor, K., and Marienau, C. "Self-Assessment: A Source for Individual and Organizational Learning." *Contemporary Education,* 1993, *64* (3), 166–169.

Thompson, K. *Learning at Evergreen (II): Writing and Thinking.* Report of the Assessment Study Group. Olympia, Wash.: Office of Research and Planning, Evergreen State College, 1992.

Viney, L. L. "A Sociophenomenological Approach to Life-Span Development Complementing Erikson's Sociodynamic Approach." *Human Development,* 1987, *30,* 125–136.

Vygotsky, L. S. *Mind in Society: The Development of Higher Psychological Processes.* Cambridge, Mass.: Harvard University Press, 1978.

Werner, H. *Developmental Processes.* In S. S. Barten and M. B. Franklin (eds.), *Selected Writings of Heinz Werner.* Vol. 1. New York: International Universities Press, 1978.

RICHARD H. HASWELL is professor of English at Washington State University.

This appendix provides examples of student self-evaluation assignments and several examples of longer self-evaluation essays and suggests additional resources on self-evaluation.

Appendix

1. Examples of Prompts and Assignments

1a. Assignment for post-writes for use in writing classes (Allen and Roswell, 1989)

Now that you have finished your essay, please answer the following questions. There are no right or wrong answers; we are interested in your analysis of your experience writing this essay.

1. What problems did you face during the writing of this essay?
2. What solutions did you find for these problems?
3. What do you think are the strengths of this essay?
4. What alternative plans for this essay did you consider? Why did you reject them?
5. Imagine you had more time to write this essay. What would you do if you were to continue working on it?

1b. Student self-evaluation essay prompt for the Measure of Intellectual Development assessment measure[1]

Look back on your experiences in [this program], and reflect on your discoveries about yourself as a learner. Please be as specific and concrete as possible about what stood out for you about this program; we want you to go into as much detail as you think is necessary to give us a clear idea of your learnings in [this program]. For example, you might want to discuss any or all of the following topics: the content/subject matter, the kinds of teachers and teaching you experienced, the classroom atmosphere, and/or the evaluation procedures that were used. Through these experiences, what have you learned about yourself as a learner?

1c. Assignment for the final essay to accompany the writing portfolio assignment, used in the Interdisciplinary Writing Program at the University of Washington[2]

Planning Your Portfolio. Toward the end of the quarter you will create a portfolio of your work to represent you as a writer participating in the discipline of geography. *Everything* you write this quarter is eligible for inclusion in your portfolio. This includes the three major essays, journal entries, peer reviews, other in-class or overnight writing assignments, and additional journal entries you generate from your own questions and reflections on writing and/or concepts and issues in development geography.

Because the portfolio is intended to be consciously and carefully selective, you should choose from six to twelve pieces of your writing. You can include more, but be sure you can explain why more pieces need to be included and why other pieces don't represent you in the way these additional pieces do.

Then write a reflective essay which creates your portfolio by integrating the pieces in the collection into a whole. Explain what the collection as a whole means to you and how this portfolio reflects you as a writer. *You* are the subject of this essay. Give attention to yourself as a writer in general and to writing in geography in particular. Discuss how you think your writing and thinking skills are related and how they may have developed or changed over the course of the quarter. Use your own writing as evidence for the arguments you want to make; discuss the meaning and value of each piece of writing selected and the relation of the pieces to one another.

Because this essay creates and explains your portfolio, it tells me how to read and evaluate your portfolio. So what you tell me the portfolio means and how seriously you take it will directly guide my evaluation and grading. (This is not the place for b.s., arguments you don't believe, or flattery.) In reviewing your portfolio I will look for the following:

- Consideration of how thinking, writing, and reading are related for you
- Evidence of critical analysis, both of your writing, that of others, and of geographic concepts
- A consideration of how disciplinary conventions shape writing in geography, hence thinking in geography
- Evidence of initiative and authority in your writing and your role as a participant in the discourse of development geography
- A consideration of how your writing is related to what you've learned in English 198C and Geography 230
- A consideration of how your writing has changed, including your understanding of your writing process, your particular style, problems, and successful strategies

1d. Prompting questions for the end-of-course SSE at Fairhaven College, Western Washington University[3]

Writing a Self-Evaluation. To be able to evaluate oneself fairly, candidly, and helpfully is a valuable life skill which will be an asset to you long after you leave college. This is perhaps the most important reason why Fairhaven requires a self-evaluation instead of a letter grade. The other reasons are that letter grades are too limited, too inaccurate, and too inflated.

There is no single way to write a good evaluation. That will depend upon the course, your goals, your style, and your needs. The advice below is only that—advice. Do not follow it slavishly or respond as if it were an outline to be followed. And do not assume that you must touch on all of the points mentioned. A good evaluation selects the most important results of the learning process, and from this selection much else is evident. Give time and thought to what you write and care to how you write. A sloppy, careless self-evaluation filled with misspellings, incomplete sentences, and half-thoughts leaves a poor final impression even if you did very well in a course of study.

A vital point: Try to write in a way which communicates information about the content of a course or independent study. Do not just speak in abstractions and personal feelings, such as "This class was extremely important to me because through discussion and the readings my thinking developed immensely." What subject? Which discussions? What did you read? think about what? developed from where to where? A reader who does not know what the class studied should be able to gain an idea from your self-evaluation. One should be able to form some judgment about how well you understand a subject from what you say about it, not merely that you claim to understand it. In other words, *be specific . . . . Be concrete.*

One of the important skills in a good education is being able to ask the right questions. Likewise, writing a good evaluation depends upon good questions. In fact, one might begin an evaluation by inquiring "What are the important questions about this subject?," listing several, and then discussing some good answers. There are many problems and issues which one might address to oneself in order to trigger a good evaluation. Here are some—suggestions only:

- Did I do more or less than was expected by the instructor? by me? Why, or why not?
- This is a _____ credit class, or about _____ of my study time this quarter. Did I give it that much time?
- What do I now understand best about this subject? least well?
- My strongest and weakest points as a student? What did I do to improve the weak points? What will I do next?
- What do I need to learn next about this subject?

- What was most satisfying about the class? most frustrating? your responsibility for each?
- Has the course irritated you? stimulated you? touched you personally? Has it made you uncomfortable about yourself, about society, about the future, about learning? Are you the same person who began the class ten weeks ago? What's different?
- What did you expect to learn? What did you actually learn? more or less, and why?

To quote former Fairhaven dean Phil Ager, "It is a fiction to measure learning in a single way which therefore can be recorded by a single letter grade." Instead, he argues, there are at least four different kinds of learning:

Cognitive. Your new understandings and knowledge? What is the most important single piece of knowledge gained? What will you remember in a year? five years? How has your knowledge grown? changed? become more sound?

Skills. New skills gained? old skills improved? your ability to solve problems, think, reason, research? Did you actually use these skills? What skills do you need to develop next?

Judgment. Do you understand the difference between process and content? Can you apply principles? to other classes? life? If you took the class again, what would you do differently? Has your way of thinking changed?

Affective (emotions and feelings). Did you change? your beliefs? values? Was the class worth your time? Do you feel good about it? the single most important thing you learned about you? Evaluate your participation in discussion. Did you discuss and learn with other students? How has the course altered your behavior? Did you grow? shrink? stagnate? float?

1e. Assignment for the quarterly student learning self-assessment at Antioch University, Seattle

In writing this assessment, include reflections on your course work, any prior learnings you have documented, and any degree-process work (degree plan documents, degree committee meetings, other portfolio documents) you did. This assessment should provide a *qualitative* reflection and analysis of your learning for the quarter. Although it is a summary of your learning, it should also be comprehensive. Above all, it should include an honest assessment of your learning and be meaningful.

1. Focus on each individual activity this quarter and briefly summarize your learning. Indicate the key ideas, insights, perspective, frameworks, or skills gained from each activity. If applicable, give an example(s) of key learning(s) which were particularly valuable to you.
2. Focus on the quarter's work as a whole. What themes, if any, emerged? What connections did you find?

3. Focus on the personal significance of the learning for you. What impact did it have on your values, belief, assumptions, or attitudes? What did it contribute to your understanding of yourself as a learner?

4. Focus on the relationship between this quarter's learning and your overall degree program. What progress did you make in relation to the goals in your area of concentration? in core purposes? other goals of your degree plan? Did your learning this quarter lead you to modify your degree plan goals? in what way? What implications for your future learning are indicated by your experience this quarter?

1f. Prompting questions for the end of the coordinated studies program at The Evergreen State College[4]

Suggestions to Students for Writing Self-Evaluations.[5] It helps to write evaluations in two stages. The first stage is really for yourself. So you can get things straight in your own head without worrying yet about what to write for the second stage: a transcript document aimed at the outside world. For the first stage, write quickly, loosely, and as much as possible without stopping. Don't even worry about mechanics, organization, or whether it makes sense. Don't even worry about whether it is true: Sometimes blatant exaggeration or distortion is the only way to get your hands on a half-buried insight. The idea is to get your thoughts and feelings down on paper where you can see them and learn from them.

Wait until *after* you get that interesting mess written before going back over it to decide which things are true and which of those true things you want to share with strangers who will read your transcript. It will be easier to write appropriately for a transcript reader when you get the false and private things down on paper so they don't make fog and static in your head to confuse and slow you down.

Save this first-stage writing for your portfolio. It will have lots of important insights that won't be in your transcript. Think about sharing much or all of it with your faculty member so as to help him or her write a better, fairer evaluation of you.

Useful Questions for Your First-Stage Self-Evaluation. [The following are useful questions when writing your first-stage self-evaluation:]

- How do you feel now at the end?
- How accurate are those feelings?
- What are you proud of?
- Compare your accomplishments with what you hoped for and expected at the start.
- Did you work hard or not? get a lot done or not?
- What kinds of things were difficult or frustrating? which were easy?
- What's the most important thing you did this period?
- What bits of reading or lecture stick in your mind?

- Think of some important moments from this learning period: your best moments, worst moments, typical moments, crises, or turning points. Tell five or six of these in a sentence or two each.
- What can you learn or did you learn from each of these moments?
- Write a letter to an important person you studied, thanking the person for what you learned. Or telling the person how you disagree. Or telling the person how good a job he or she did.
- Who is the person you studied you cared most about? BE that person and write that person's letter to you, telling you whatever it is the person has to tell you.
- What did you learn throughout? skills and ideas. What was the most important thing? What idea or skill was hardest to really "get"? What crucial idea or skill just came naturally?
- When they make the movie, who will play you? What's the movie really about?
- Describe this period as a journey: to where? what kind of terrain? Is it a complete trip or part of a longer one?
- You learned something crucial which you won't discover for a while. Guess it now.
- Tell a few ways you could have done a better job.
- What knowledge and skills will you need in five years? Did you learn any?
- What advice would some friends in the program give you if they spoke with 100 percent honesty and caring?
- What advice do you have for yourself?

Questions to Answer in Your Transcript Self-Evaluation. [The following are questions to answer when writing your transcript self-evaluation.]

What did you do? Faculty members will include an official program description as part of your transcript, so you don't need to tell the core activities and reading. Just say whether you did them and go on to tell briefly the things you did that weren't part of the required core. Which activities were most important to you? You can cover this whole question briefly in a few sentences unless there is some complicating factor or a special reason to go into more detail.

What did you learn? skills and content. This is probably the main thing they need to know. And you probably know more than your teacher about what you learned. Tell a whole bunch of things briefly—perhaps just a list of bare phrases. But then zero in on at least one or two important ideas or skills and tell about them in some detail. In effect, this part of your evaluation is a micro-essay—only a paragraph or two—that *explains* something you know. The bare list of things you learned is a *telling* to the readers, which they must take on faith; here you are *showing* readers something you know and thereby proving it.

What was the learning process like for you?

What does it all add up to for you? Where did you come from, and where are you going?

Things to Keep in Mind. You are writing for strangers and officials: employers or admissions officers or faculty members at another school. Writing to official strangers sometimes freezes the words inside you so you can't write at all or else turns them to plastic so they come out all fake, bureaucratic, and untrustworthy. It may help to write as though you are writing a letter to a friend, loved one, teacher, or yourself. This will not only help you to write more easily, it will also help your writing have some voice and sound like it comes from a real person. In revising, you can make whatever small changes may be necessary to fit your official audience but still keep the real voice in your writing. Illustrate your generalizations with brief examples. You can get an event into half a sentence ("such as when I . . ."). Tell things you are proud of. If you cannot think of any, think again. They are there. But also try to describe those parts of your performance that you are not satisfied with, or things you need to work on in the future, or things you would have done differently if you knew then what you know now. You are likely to sound dumb or dishonest if you cannot think of *some* things you could do better on the basis of experience.

Don't complain about how terrible the program or teachers were. It'll just sound like sour grapes and make readers think you blame things on others and don't accept responsibility for your own learning. Save those complaints for evaluations of program and faculty. If the complaints keep sneaking into your self-evaluation, stop and do a draft of your program and faculty evaluations. Get the complaints out of your system so you can focus your energies on what counts here: your learning.

Keep it short. Most transcript readers won't be used to reading these long, complicated Evergreen transcripts and will be in a hurry. Cut out what isn't crucial. Tell the readers that if they want to know more, you have a portfolio to show them with longer descriptions of your learning and examples of your actual work. (And make sure you have one.) But don't be afraid to let them get a feel of you. You will come across strongest if you come across real. They need to trust you. The best way I know is to try hard for the real truth and to let yourself sound like a real person.

Don't type your transcript evaluation on the official form without getting feedback on a draft of it from your faculty member and at least one other student: What seems right and wrong? How does the writing strike them? The best way to get feedback is to get them to describe the person they find in the self-evaluation. Get them also to help you with awkward writing and mistakes in mechanics. When you finally type it on the official form be sure to proofread it carefully and get someone else who is a good proofreader. Some transcript readers will be more influenced by mistakes in mechanics and typing and messiness than by anything else.

1g. Prompting questions for the end-of-undergraduate-career Summary and Evaluation document at Fairhaven College, Western Washington University[6]

Writing Your Summary and Evaluation. Here are some questions and exercises to "prime the pump" for the Summary and Evaluation (S&E) paper. You do not need to answer all these questions to write a good paper; however, you may want to think about each of these prior to beginning. Some tips: use concrete examples; remember the S&E is not a litany of all the classes you have taken but a discussion of how the classes and their themes are related and/or how a particular line of questioning was followed.

- What is the strongest component of your education (qualitative, not necessarily quantitative)?
- If you were designing your concentration again (or if you had the choice to revise your major), what would you change? Why?
- Describe your new understanding and knowledge. How has your knowledge grown? What will you remember in a year? five years?
- What do you still need to know?
- What is the theory, guiding principle, or philosophy that shaped your education?
- What is the relationship between theory and practice in your work?
- What are the critical issues in your disciplines/academic program? How did the disciplines you chose to study (or the choices made in your major) help you ask these important questions?
- How does your concentration/major look in terms of breadth and depth? Did you sacrifice one for the other?
- How does your education help you answer ethical and moral questions?
- What "useful" skills have you learned? Did you gain skills in the ability to solve problems, think, reason, research? What skills do you need to develop next?
- What role did [this college] play in your education?
- Did you miss segments of learning at [this college]? Did you find areas of learning that you couldn't have found in other places?
- Is there a "most important thing" you've learned in college? What is it?
- What do you hope to be doing ten to fifteen years from now? In what ways will your "education" help you get there?
- What have been your strongest and weakest points as a student? What did you do to improve your weaker areas? What will you do next?

2. Examples of Longer Student Self-Evaluation Essays

2a. SSE to accompany a writing portfolio

Portfolio Essay Written in Response to 1c. As I thought about how I wanted to approach this essay and skimmed through the various pieces that I have written this quarter I realized that it was going to be quite a challenge to put this portfolio together. I knew deep down that my writing had developed substantially throughout the quarter, but how to best present this both in words and in a collection of written pieces was causing me some problems. I finally realized that the best way to represent my internal changes with the writing process would be to . . . put together a portfolio of pieces which had a clear, distinctive link to one another. I felt that this would be best accomplished by choosing several pieces that spanned the entire development of my news analysis assignment.

Analysis of these pieces has opened my eyes to the fact that I have become much more adept at intertwining critical thinking, the use of previous and newly acquired knowledge, and an incorporation of a geographic mind-set to effectively present my research and ideas on paper. . . . At each stage I have thought out how I could present something more effectively, what relevance or place my own critical analysis and/or research had with the problem and solutions I was trying to present, and what I could learn from a critique of other peoples' writing. I also was constantly reading, whether it was going through an article for the fifth time trying to find that critical piece of evidence or skimming through one of my drafts again to look for places it did not flow very well. Finally, I was writing, not only the actual drafts but also the news article summaries, the peer responses, the personal evaluations, and the journal entries that helped me pull all my ideas together between one draft and the next. This whole process also helped me realize not only the complexities of dealing with a geographic problem, but also the importance of studying them. . . .

I begin with my prospectus for essay #2. This is the piece that got everything started. I nailed down the topic that I wanted to spend the next several weeks developing, and I also began to shape what angle I wanted to approach it from. This piece shows how, despite the fact that I had yet to do any research, I was using previous knowledge to begin to explore a geographic problem.

My second piece is journal entry #5. This piece shows a clear link between reading articles and analyzing their relevance or importance. It is here where I truly begin to develop what would become a very important issue for my topic—the many different perspectives and biases that must be taken into account when discussing a geographical problem. As I write in my answer to question #3, "I would probably, in my case, expect the issues to be presented in a pro-U.S., anti-drug manner. Alternate conceptualizations of the issues could easily be seen since there are so many other parties . . . involved." I laugh as I read this now, because I did not realize back then how very complicated this could make things.

My third piece is my first news article summary. This represents the beginning of my research and the important process of transforming something that I read into relevant writing. This particular piece first opened a very important discussion my essays needed to include, that of the urban connections of the drug trade, and through careful reading I was able to make this connection.

My fourth piece is my rough draft for essay #2. . . . . This draft exhibits not only two of the most important aspects of my development of the news analysis assignment, that of urban and international links and the use of different perspectives, but also some of the problems I would have to work through. . . .

My sixth piece of writing is my self-evaluation for essay #2. This represents the use of my analysis of my own writing to help move toward the incorporation of solutions into my essay. . . .

My eighth piece of writing is my answer to the journal question for essay #3. This represents how I have developed an ability to look beyond the scope of my own paper and discuss different approaches I might have taken to it. It also shows how incorporating another person's ideas of geographic research can be a very enriching experience. . . .

My ninth piece of writing is my final draft of paper #3. . . . As I have said in my self-evaluation, "As the paper progresses from draft to draft less important information is dropped and pertinent info is emphasized and made clearer. The organization of the paper also becomes stronger." This draft is the result of a continual process of reading, writing, and thinking. I have taken what initially seemed to be a simple geographic problem, researched it, analyzed it, and wrote about it until I felt I had produced an end product that clearly represented, explained, and discussed the problem and its solutions. My choice of the coca industry in Peru not only challenged me, but its complexity helped me develop my overall analytical writing ability.

In conclusion, this sequence of pieces represents not only the sequence of development that my writing has gone through this quarter in general, but also the development it has gone through in a geographic sense. I have realized the complexities of writing about a problem that at times seemed rather irrelevant to my own life, and through a continual process of rethinking, doing more research, and then revising my ideas I have simplified those complexities and produced something I could be proud to share. Along the way I have also learned another important lesson—that problems in other parts of the world and their connections to the world I live in are well worth studying. Looking at such problems not only taught me the importance of looking at this world and its inhabitants as one whole, but also the importance of thoughtfully representing the views and plights of others in a relatively unbiased fashion. I am now ready to carry this new attitude into my future writings, both in geography and wherever else it may apply.

2b. Two SSEs written by the same student at The Evergreen State College

Self-Evaluation, "Foundations of Human Expression" Program, 1984–85. Upon entering the Foundations of Human Expression in September, my main goals were to improve my writing skills, reading skills, and learn some new insights into performing. I have achieved improvements in these areas, particularly the reading and writing skills. This program has also helped me gain insight into new areas of art perception, creation, and religion from the books we were required to read. My reading and writing skills improved in the winter quarter. I had completed all but five of the required readings in the fall quarter due to poor time management; I completed all readings in the winter quarter. I completed all writing assignments and attended all lectures and seminars.

Throughout this program, I have become aware of skills that I have achieved and improved, and skills that I need to work on as well. These skills were brought out by attending workshops, module classes, and seminars. In the program workshops, dealing with sound and rhythm, movement, expository writing and creative writing, increased or introduced an awareness in these areas. I took two module classes, one in modern dance and one in ballet. These classes aided my abilities in different areas of dance, as did the African drumming and dancing workshops at the program retreat. These workshops provided at the retreat taught me new cultural ideas also, as did the Native American wood carving and Asian/American theatre workshops. In seminar, I have discovered I need improvement on my speaking skills, and though I have improved in the winter quarter, I still need work in that area.

This program dealt quite a lot with performance. Each time I performed in front of an audience, it was a good learning experience. During such performances as sound and movement workshops, I learned about improvising within a structure, which I hadn't dealt with before. I also performed once or twice in my module classes. These presentations helped prepare me for the program's final presentations, and such experiences aided me in achieving a successful performance.

After this program, I have several ideas about what I will do later in my education. I intend to work on my fear of speaking my mind in a group situation. I also wish to explore new forms of self-expression, art, and stage performance. This program has opened that up for me.

Student Self-Evaluation, "American Worlds, Democratic Vistas" Program, 1987–88. This past spring quarter in "American Worlds, Democratic Vistas" has marked my last quarter of four years at Evergreen. I have come to learn a great deal in these last three quarters, particularly about new ways of looking at history and an understanding of what democracy really means, at least to me.

I feel that, in this past year, over the course of the program. I have become more comfortable with the content of the work and have improved my own academic skills as well. My participation in seminar has not been great, but I feel I have made progress, particularly from fall quarter. I enjoyed the seminars and the reading materials most of all. We were given a well-mixed supply of books, written both by historians and novelists. It was from reading these that

I got a new idea of how to look at history. Before, I had always accepted books by bona fide historians as the only way to read true and accurate history, and had never seriously thought to read historical fiction to get a better feeling for the past than a history book could give. However, in winter quarter, when we started reading such novels as Mark Twain's *Adventures of Huckleberry Finn* and moved on to William Faulkner's *Absalom, Absalom!*, I found myself enjoying them and recognizing them as relevant historical accounts, sometimes giving a more realistic view of what was going on than a textbook might. I also found that some of the historians' work, such as Lawrence Goodwyn's *The Populist Moment,* Studs Terkel's *Hard Times,* and Derrick Bell's *And We Are Not Saved* were enjoyable in a lot of the same ways I found the literature enjoyable. These authors found an interesting and unique way of examining their historical subjects, using characters and real situations to make their work more compelling. I feel that reading such books as these gave me new ideas as to how to read and understand history.

I have also come to have a more solid idea of what "democracy" might mean, and this idea was one I got from reading Goodwyn's *The Populist Moment.* Prior to this class, I had always seen democracy as a governmental term, used to define the United States. Democracy was always used as something that was positive, and better than communism or socialism. Other than that as American, we were all living in a democracy, I never really thought about it beyond that. In *The Populist Moment,* Goodwyn related the story of the revolt of a group of poor farmers, whose purpose was to change and improve their lives. This idea, of the people of the country being able to gather and work together to change their way of life, is what I think democracy is all about. Democracy is essentially about the people, not a term used by the government to show how much better we are than communists.

The most substantial work that was done consistently throughout this year was undoubtedly the research. For my own project, I chose to do something related to John C. Calhoun and his pre–Civil War activities. I had some difficulty focusing my topic, but finally I decided to look at how northern historians and southern historians treated the Calhoun legend and see how they contrasted. The most notable contrast I found was that the southern expressed much more admiration for the honor and nobility of Calhoun's character than the northerners did. In working on this paper, I found that a lot of reading historians' books is merely reading the historians' own opinion. It is hard to determine what might be the truth about what happened in the past, and nearly impossible to find any author who is absolutely objective.

I feel that this program has been a good one to finish my undergraduate college years. I feel that this school has taught me how to think more analytically, see more than one side of an issue, and how to listen to others and benefit from their insights and knowledge. I think this class, more so than any of the others, has helped me realize these things, things that I can take with me and help me in the future.

2c. Summary and Evaluation paper, Fairhaven College, Western Washington University

Summary and Evaluation. My academic direction developed from a desire to learn how attitudes about race and gender roles are incorporated into U.S. governmental, economic and cultural systems, and how in turn, these social systems affect the lives of racial minorities and women. This provided an impetus for the major questions in my concentration: (1) How have the experiences of racial minorities and women influenced social institutions? (2) What methods have racial minorities and women used to influence values embodied in social structures, such as individual rights, liberty, equality, and equal opportunity? (3) Historically, how have racial minorities and women responded to social institutions, that is, by assimilation, redefinition, or rejection? (4) How have racial minorities and women been perceived by the dominant culture and how do racial minorities and women perceive themselves? By answering these questions and their subsequent corollaries, I hoped to gain the knowledge and skills to analyze, critique and contribute to society in a positive manner.

I approached the concentration with a strong feminist, race and class (economic) consciousness and combined several disciplines to draw on a variety of perspectives. History, political science, cross-cultural studies, economics and literature contribute specific information to help build a broader understanding of the topics explored. For example, knowledge of political and economic systems, of values and belief systems that determine direction, provides insight into the whys and hows of historical events and eras. Cross-cultural studies, with a focus on differing cultural traditions, help one understand how different racial groups interact with the dominant cultural systems. Literature that explores the experiences of racial minorities and women provides a special kind of insight. It is a valuable and enjoyable way to learn what issues were important in a given era, how they were perceived and reactions they induced. For example, the novel, *Uncle Tom's Cabin,* published in 1852 by Harriet Beecher Stowe, is a personal commentary about the institution of slavery and its social ramifications. Social theory, cross-cultural studies and history can be used to analyze the accuracy and impact of this novel as written by an upper-class, northern, white woman. It provides one angle from which to examine social attitudes about slavery and the impact slavery had on society.

Although exploring overall experiences of racial minorities and women, I have concentrated on studying the historical and contemporary experience of Afro-American women. This focus led to the development of my senior project: team teaching a seminar on the "History of Afro-American Women." Researching, designing and teaching this seminar forced continual evaluation of the objectives and progress of the concentration. Examples of all class materials—bibliographies, syllabus, topic questions, handouts, reading lists, assignments—as well as self and student evaluations were compiled for distribution to seminar advisers and inclusion in my academic file.

My education provided skills to address questions in my concentration. For example, reading theory in political science or economics continually tested my ability to comprehend and analyze difficult material. That exposure has raised the level of thinking and opened new avenues of information. The way in which I approach historical material has also been transformed. I no longer consider history to be just the memorization of names, dates, and events. It is also important to raise questions about the material in terms of who wrote it, for what purpose, from what perspective; what issues and people were left out of the account; and in what context the material was presented. Answering these questions about any historical account can shed a light remarkably different from convention. My ability to find and utilize information is another area which has progressed through my academic career. Building class assignments and finding information for the seminar sharpened skills on how to use libraries, bibliographies and indexes.

The main area where I lack confidence is in communication. To communicate effectively, orally or in writing, is crucial to the application of my education. Future plans include both postgraduate study and work in organizations that seek to address issues concerning the position of racial minorities and women in U.S. social institutions. The ability to affect social policy requires skillful communication.

A strength of my concentration lies in its diversity. The interdisciplinary approach exposed me to a variety of theories about social systems and how they relate to people. This diversity means knowing a little about a lot of subjects, yet it left me with strong perspectives from which to consider the experience and condition of racial minorities and women. In addition, by focusing on Afro-American women, I leave this phase of my education with a sense of having a "specialty," one area where I have gained more than general knowledge.

3. Additional Resources

Theoretical works that support student development and the value of self-reflection

Belenky, M. F., Clinchy, B. M., Goldberger, N. R., and Tarule, J. M. *Women's Ways of Knowing: The Development of Self, Voice, and Mind.* New York: Basic Books, 1986.
    Based on in-depth conversations with women, refines and extends William Perry's work on intellectual development, and offers a valuable array of ideas for collaborative learning in the service of more inclusive teaching and learning environments.

Bruner, J. *Actual Minds, Possible Worlds.* Cambridge, Mass.: Harvard University Press, 1986.
    Offers an impressive analysis of personal development, modes of thinking, and cultural change. One chapter ("The Transactional Self") is devoted to self-reflection, and another ("The Language of Education") is devoted to teaching.

Chickering, A. W., and Reisser, L. *Education and Identity.* (2nd ed.) San Francisco: Jossey-Bass, 1993.

Conceptualizes student development along seven vectors: developing competence, managing emotions, moving through autonomy toward independence, developing mature interpersonal relationships, establishing identity, developing purpose, and developing integrity; updated and expanded version of the 1969 edition.

Dewey, J. *Experience and Education.* New York: Collier, 1938.

Asserts that ability is developed by learning to reflect on one's experience; explores the connections among reflecting, learning from experience, and developing the capacity for democratic citizenship.

Kegan, R. *The Evolving Self.* Cambridge, Mass.: Harvard University Press, 1982.

Describes a general developmental model, with acknowledged influences from William Perry's and Carole Gilligan's related but more specific efforts and with a conceptual framework for the conditions involved in how people move (or can be encouraged to move) through their developmental journey; clearly emphasizes community and collaboration.

Knowles, M. *The Adult Learner: A Neglected Species.* (3rd ed.) Houston, Tex.: Gulf Publishing, 1984.

Proposes "andragogy," a theory of adult learning that focuses on linking learning and experience, adopting problem-centered teaching, and developing the skills of lifelong, self-directed learning.

Kolb, D. A. *Experiential Learning: Experience as the Source of Learning and Development.* Englewood Cliffs, N.J.: Prentice Hall, 1984.

Draws on the work of Dewey, Lewin, and Piaget to propose a model of learning that balances experience, reflection, and the formation and testing of abstract concepts and ideas.

Perry, W. G. *Forms of Intellectual and Ethical Development in the College Years: A Scheme.* Troy, Mo.: Holt, Rinehart & Winston, 1970.

Defines a developmental model of college students that has proved to be a powerful influence on an enormous range of subsequent work related to the college years. It remains, with Dewey's and Whitehead's work, one of the most significant theoretical foundations of collaborative learning efforts, as well as one of the best examples of in-depth research on students' reflections about their learning.

Rogers, C. R. *Freedom to Learn.* Columbus, Ohio: Merrill, 1969.

Explores the qualities of the relationship necessary for effective learning in educational settings, including trust, mutual respect, shared excitement, and curiosity; proposes the concept of teacher as facilitator of learning.

Schön, D. A. *Educating the Reflective Practitioner: Toward a New Design for Teaching and Learning in the Professions.* San Francisco: Jossey-Bass, 1987.

Argues for educating people to practice skilled reflection-in-action ("thinking what they are doing while they are doing it"), which is so often required in addressing complex and uncertain situations in professional settings.

Whitehead, A. N. *The Aims of Education and Other Essays.* New York: Mentor Books, 1949. (Originally published 1929.)

Emphasizes the development of imagination, creativity, and an aesthetic sense; stresses the importance of vitality both in the teacher and in the teacher-student relationship.

Practical approaches and studies relating specifically to student self-evaluation

Allen, M. S., and Roswell, B. S. "Self-Evaluation as Holistic Assessment." Paper presented at the annual meeting of the Conference on College Composition and Communication, Seattle, Wash., Mar. 1989. (ED 303 809).

Presents an overview of writing assessment through the vehicle of "postwrites," short self-assessments turned in with each writing assignment.

Alverno College Assessment Council. "Self Assessment: Summary Report." Milwaukee, Wis.: Alverno College Productions, 1989.

Offers findings that compare beginning students' ability to assess their own work with those of more advanced students.

Angelo, T. A., and Cross, K. P. *Classroom Assessment Techniques: A Handbook for College Teachers.* (2nd ed.) San Francisco: Jossey-Bass, 1993.

Presents a wealth of approaches to in-class assessments of students (including ones that focus on self-assessment) that can inform the teaching process.

Sommers, J. "The Writer's Memo: Collaboration, Response, and Development." In C. M. Anson (ed.), *Writing and Response: Theory, Practice, Research.* Urbana, Ill.: National Council of Teachers of English, 1989.

Introduces another version of self-assessment to accompany writing assignments.

Thompson, K. *Learning at Evergreen: An Assessment of Cognitive Development.* Washington Center for Undergraduate Education Monograph, no. 1. Olympia, Wash.: Evergreen State College, 1991.

Presents the results of a ground-breaking study analyzing a large sample of formal student self-evaluation documents for longitudinal evidence of intellectual development at a single institution in Washington State.

Thompson, K. *Learning at Evergreen (II): Writing and Thinking.* Report of the Assessment Study Group. Olympia, Wash.: Office of Research and Planning, Evergreen State College, 1992.

Expands and summarizes earlier assessment work using formal institutional student self-evaluation documents, which were analyzed for composition, communication, and cognitive complexity, separately and through a single combined index.

Wolf, D. P. "Assessment as an Episode of Learning." In R. Bennett and W. Ward (eds.), *Construction Versus Choice in Cognitive Measurement.* New York: Erlbaum, 1993.

Argues compellingly for changing the culture of testing to one of assessment, with episodes "in which both students and teachers learn about the standards of good work and how to achieve them"; presents a model for assessment built on continuous performance and response.

Notes

1. Contributed by William S. Moore, Center for the Study of Intellectual Development, 1505 Farwell Court NW, Olympia, WA 98502.
2. Contributed by Kim Johnson-Bogart, Center for Instructional Development and Research, University of Washington, Seattle, WA 98195.
3. Written by Don McLeod, member of the faculty, and widely used at Fairhaven College, Western Washington University, Bellingham, Wash.
4. Written in 1978 by Peter Elbow while he was a member of the faculty at The Evergreen State College, Olympia, Wash., and widely used at the college since.
5. The Evergreen State College Student Self-Evaluation is a formal document suggested but not required in Evergreen students' transcripts.
6. Contributed by Marie Eaton, Dean, Fairhaven College, Western Washington University, Bellingham, Wash.

Reference

Allen, M. S., and Roswell, B. S. "Self-Evaluation as Holistic Assessment." Paper presented at the annual meeting of the Conference on College Composition and Communication, Seattle, Wash., March 1989. (ED 303 809).

INDEX

Accountability, higher education, 58
Allen, M. S., 17
Alverno College, 78
Alverno College Assessment Council, 38
Angelo, T. A., 16, 45, 69
Antioch University (Seattle), 6–8, 27, 43, 104–105
Arlin, P. K., 92
Assessment: and Measure of Intellectual Development, 75–76, 101; and student self-evaluations, 43–44. *See also* Evaluation; Grading; Outcomes assessment; Testing
Association of American Colleges, 66
. Astin, A., 40, 52, 66
Attinasi, L., 69
Authority, 58–59
Autonomy, 55–56
Avens, C., 75

Basseches, M., 86
Bearison, D. J., 92
Bee, H. L., 92
Belenky, M. F., 10, 12, 27, 36, 54
Ben-Ur, T., 68–69
Benack, S., 95
Beyer, C., 73
Bloom, B., 12
Bown, H. R., 66
Broad learning outcomes, 70–72
Brown, A. L., 85, 86
Bruner, J., 87, 94

California Assessment Program (CAP), 72

Capstone courses, 29–30
Case, R., 85
Centralia College (Washington), 21
Change: and developmental episodes, 86; frame, 86; and learning, 11; teaching, 61–62
Chickering, A. W., 85, 92, 96
Claxton, C. S., 27
Clinchy, B. M., 10, 12, 27, 36, 54
Coercion, 86, 88, 98
Cohler, B. J., 92
College. *See* Higher education
Community: defined, 52; learning, 23–24,

52; and student self-evaluations, 52–54; teacher-student, 46
Conflict. *See* Frame change/conflict
Coordinated students, 24–27
Critical thinking: skills, 12; student, 10; and student self-evaluation, 20, 22. *See also* Problem solving
Cross, K. P., 16, 45, 69
Cross, S., 95

Deemer, D., 68–69
Development: academic perspective, 93; assessment, 74–77; cognitive/affective, 56; defined, 84–85; and instruction, 85; intellectual, 12–13; and learning, 11–13; life-span/adult, 92–93, 96–97; and maturity, 84; postsecondary, 92–93; and student self-evaluations, 45, 94–97; theoretical works, 114–116. *See also* Developmental episodes
Developmental activity, 90–91
Developmental episodes: and coercion, 86, 99, 98; and embeddedness, 86, 88, 90; and experiential learning, 88; and frame change, 86, 88, 90–92; and integration, 87, 89, 97–98; and known sequence, 87, 89; and life history, 87, 89; and self-reflection, 86–87, 88–89; and student self-evaluations, 88–97; traits, 86–87; and vacillation, 86, 88, 91
Developmental language, 91–92
Dewey, J., 12, 90

Eaton, M., 70, 77
Eaton, M. D., 29
Edmonds Community College (Seattle), 16–17
Education: beyond-discipline, 47–48; and development, 85; and self-reflection, 5; as utilizing knowledge, 5, 13. *See also* Higher education
Educational Testing Service (ETS), 72–73
Elbow, P., 50
Embeddedness, 86, 88, 90
Evaluation. *See* Assessment; Self-evaluation; Student self-evaluation; Student self-evaluations (SSEs)
Evergreen State College, The, 19, 25–26,

interdisciplinary, program, 23–24, 102; peer, groups, 24; portfolios, 72–73, 102, 108–110; post, 16–17, 101; problems, 37–38; reflective, 72; self-reflective, 49–50; student self-evaluations, 6, 35–45, 103–104, 105, 108; and thinking, 73–73. *See also* Student self-evaluations (SSEs)

Yakima Valley Community College, 20

Zelley, R., 75
Zimiles, H., 92

ORDERING INFORMATION

NEW DIRECTIONS FOR TEACHING AND LEARNING is a series of paperback books that presents ideas and techniques for improving college teaching, based both on the practical expertise of seasoned instructors and on the latest research findings of educational and psychological researchers. Books in the series are published quarterly in Spring, Summer, Fall, and Winter and are available for purchase by subscription as well as by single copy.

SUBSCRIPTIONS for 1993 cost $47.00 for individuals (a savings of 20 percent over single-copy prices) and $62.00 for institutions, agencies, and libraries. Please do not send institutional checks for personal subscriptions. Standing orders are accepted.

SINGLE COPIES cost $15.95 when payment accompanies order. (California, New Jersey, New York, and Washington, D.C., residents please include appropriate sales tax.) Billed orders will be charged postage and handling.

DISCOUNTS FOR QUANTITY ORDERS are available. Please write to the address below for information.

ALL ORDERS must include either the name of an individual or an official purchase order number. Please submit your order as follows:
    Subscriptions: specify series and year subscription is to begin
    Single copies: include individual title code (such as TL1)

MAIL ALL ORDERS TO:
    Jossey-Bass Publishers
    350 Sansome Street
    San Francisco, California 94104-1342

FOR SINGLE-COPY SALES OUTSIDE OF THE UNITED STATES CONTACT:
    Maxwell Macmillan International Publishing Group
    866 Third Avenue
    New York, New York 10022-6221

FOR SUBSCRIPTION SALES OUTSIDE OF THE UNITED STATES, CONTACT:
    any international subscription agency or Jossey-Bass directly.

OTHER TITLES AVAILABLE IN THE
NEW DIRECTIONS FOR TEACHING AND LEARNING SERIES
Robert J. Menges, Editor-in-Chief
Marilla D. Svinicki, Associate Editor